ON THE DEMOCRATIC IDEA IN AMERICA

ON THE

HARPER & ROW, PUBLISHERS

New York, Evanston, San Francisco, London

1817

DEMOCRATIC IDEA
IN AMERICA

Irving Kristol

The material in this book originally appeared in the following publications:

"Urban Civilization and Its Discontents" in *Commentary*, Vol. 50, No. 1 (July 1970).

"The Shaking of the Foundations" in *Fortune*, July 1968.

"Pornography, Obscenity, and the Case for Censorship" in *The New York Times Magazine*, March 28, 1971.

"American Historians and the Democratic Idea" in *The American Scholar*, Vol. 39, No. 1 (Winter 1969–70).

"American Intellectuals and Foreign Policy" in *Foreign Affairs*, July 1967. Copyright © 1967 by The Council on Foreign Relations, Inc. Reprinted by permission of *Foreign Affairs*.

"When Virtue Loses All Her Loveliness" in *The Public Interest*, No. 21 (Fall 1970).

"Toward a Restructuring of the University" in *The New York Times Magazine*, December 8, 1968.

"Utopianism and American Politics" appeared in *The New York Times Magazine*, November 14, 1971 issue, under the title "A Foolish American Ism—Utopianism."

STANDARD BOOK NUMBER: 06-012467-9

LIBRARY OF CONGRESS CATALOG CARD NUMBER: 76-178731

Contents

For my father, Joseph Kristol

Preface

THESE ESSAYS were written and published over the past five years and, except for the correction of a couple of factual errors and the elimination of a few topical references, they are here reprinted without revision. Though composed for different occasions, they do overlap—and, in a sense, these overlappings are what each of the essays is really "about." They suggest a common theme and a common concern: the tendency of democratic republics to depart from—to "progress" away from, one might say—their original, animating principles, and as a consequence to precipitate grave crises in the moral and political order.

In the United States, these original principles firmly linked popular government to a fair measure of self-government (i.e., self-discipline) on the part of the individual citizen. The departure from these principles has taken the form of a "liberation" of personal and collective selves—a freeing of self-interests, personal aspirations, private fantasies—in the realms of economics, politics, education, and culture. It is assumed, on the basis of various benign theories about human nature and human history, that the actions of self-serving men will coalesce into a common good, and that the emancipation of the individual from social restraints will result in a more perfect community. I do think that, within limits, the notion of the "hidden hand" has its uses in the marketplace, which is the domain of "economic men" rather than of citizens, and where the specter of bankruptcy does impose a kind of self-discipline. I believe the results are disastrous when it is extended to the polity as a whole, which can go bankrupt only once, and whose destiny is finally determined by the capacity of its citizenry to govern its passions and thereby rightly understand its enduring common interests.

This theme and this problem imposed themselves upon my thinking gradually. Like all Americans, I was born into the ideology of liberal democracy, in its twentieth-century version, as into a civil religion; I therefore found it extremely difficult to ascribe any of the problems of our nation to the problematics inherent in this ideological conception of itself. Not only did that seem un-American; it is, in fact, quite un-American. I had to discover for myself, uneasily and fumblingly, many things which a serious student of political philosophy—someone soundly versed in Aristotle's *Politics*, for example—might have known early on. But since there are so few students of political philosophy from whom one can learn these days, I should like to think this effort at self-education was perhaps not entirely wasted and that others may possibly find something instructive in it.

A question that is bound to be raised in our overheated political climate is: do these essays add up to anything that can be called "a political position"? The candid answer is, alas, an equivocal one. It is fairly clear, I would hope, that I am not comfortable with what passes for either liberalism or conservatism in the United States today. My instincts are—I have in-

deed come to believe that an adult's "normal" political instincts should be—conservative: I have observed over the years
that the unanticipated consequences of social action are always
more important, and usually less agreeable, than the intended
consequences. I also regard the exaggerated hopes we attach
to politics as the curse of our age, just as I regard moderation
as one of our vanishing virtues. But I also believe that many of
our institutions—political, economic, educational—have been
so debased as to need substantial reformation, not only to survive but to merit survival. And I should like to see such
reforms carried out by moderate men, using moderate means.
This is not an obviously secure position, but neither is it, I
would insist, a completely unrealistic one. It does seem to me
that some of our most admirable American statesmen can be
said to have been engaged in exactly such an enterprise of conservative reform, and that this political tradition is still available to us.

The two contemporary thinkers who have most shaped my
own thought, not necessarily in ways they would always approve of, are Lionel Trilling and Leo Strauss. I should like to
take this opportunity to thank them for being there. I have
also benefited from conversations, over these past three
decades, with my wife, Gertrude Himmelfarb, and my good
friends, Daniel Bell and Martin Diamond. None of my specific
opinions is to be imputed to them, but I should be unhappy if
they did not find some merit in my views, even when we are
in less than perfect agreement.

1

Urban Civilization and Its Discontents

IT IS IN THE NATURE of democratic countries that, sooner or later, all serious controversy—whether it be political, social, or economic—will involve an appeal to the democratic principle as the supreme arbiter of the rights and the wrongs of the affair. One might begin by invoking the idea of justice, or liberty, or equity, or natural rights; but in the end what is unjust or illiberal or unnatural—or even what is simply "un-American"—will be defined in terms of what is most properly democratic. It follows, therefore, that to the extent to which our idea of democracy is vague or unrealistic or self-contradictory, we shall be less able to resolve the issues that divide us.

I do not mean, of course, that a neat and precise and generally accepted definition of democracy will in and of itself automatically pacify the body politic and avoid bitter conflicts of interests and values. There is no magic in ideas, even when we superstitiously attribute a quasi-divine authority to them. But ideas do give shape to our sentiments, our consciences, and our moral energies. And a muddled idea can, in time, give birth

Adapted from the inaugural lecture as Henry Luce Professor of Urban Values, New York University, April 1970.

to some fairly grotesque political realities. One has only to re-call that, for nearly a century after the formation of the American republic, it was widely accepted that our idea of democracy for all was compatible with a condition of slavery for some, to realize that this is no mere abstract possibility. And the fact that it required a bloody civil war to establish what the authentic intentions of our democracy were would indicate that—as in certain older theological controversies that disrupted the real world of Christendom—the precise meaning of the democratic dogma can have the most material bearing upon the kind of society we live in and the ways in which we live in it.

At the moment, for example, we are all of us much exer-cised about the quality of life in our American urban civiliza-tion. I have no intention, at this time, of analyzing the numer-ous problems which make up what we familiarly call the "crisis of our cities." Instead, I should like to focus on the apparent incapacity of our democratic and urban civiliza-tion to come to grips with these problems. In other words, if it is proper to say that we experience the crisis of our cities, it is equally proper to say that we *are* the urban crisis. And what I want to suggest further is that one of the main reasons we are so problematic to ourselves is the fact that we are creating a democratic, urban civilization while stubbornly refusing to think clearly about the relation of urbanity to democracy.

In this respect, we are far removed indeed from the found-ing fathers of this republic, who thought deeply about this re-lationship—but in a way so uncongenial to us that we find it most difficult to take their thinking seriously. We even find it difficult to study their thinking fairly. Thus, in the many books that have appeared in recent years surveying the history of the American city and of American attitudes toward the city, we usually find a discussion of the "agrarian bias" of the founding fathers. More often than not, this is taken quite simply to mean that their opinions were an unreflective expression of their rural condition: a provincial prejudice, familiar enough—the antagonism of country to town is no new thing—and understandable enough in human terms, but now to be regarded as rather quaint and entirely unilluminating. I think that this approach is not only an obstacle to our understanding the American past; it also represents a lost opportunity for us to take our bearings in the present.

To take such a bearing, we ought to begin with an appreciation of the fact that the ideas of the founding fathers did not, in their sum, amount to an agrarian *bias* so much as an anti-urban *philosophy;* which is to say, the founding fathers had reasons for thinking as they did, and until we consider these reasons and come to terms with them, we are more likely to be living testimony to the validity of their apprehensions than to the presumed anachronistic character of these apprehensions.

The founding fathers saw democracy in America as resting upon two major pillars. The first, whose principles and rationale are so superbly set forth in the *Federalist Papers,* was the "new science of government" which made popular government possible in a large and heterogeneous republic. This "new science" designed a machinery of self-government that has to be considered as one of the most remarkable political inventions of Western man. The machinery is by now familiar to us; representative and limited government, separation of powers; majority rule but refined so that it had to express the will of various majorities elected in various ways; a diffusion of political and economic power which would thwart the intentions of any single-minded faction no matter how large and influential, and so on and so forth. The basic idea behind all these arrangements was that the pursuit of self-interest was the most reliable of human motivations on which to build a political system—but this pursuit had to be, to use one of their favorite phrases, the pursuit of self-interest "rightly understood," and such "right understanding" needed the benevolent, corrective checks and balances of the new political machinery to achieve decent self-definition—i.e., to converge at a point of common weal.

The second pillar envisaged by the founding fathers was of a spiritual order—and the fact that most of us today prefer to call it "psychological" rather than spiritual would have been taken by them as itself a clear sign of urban decadence. To designate this pillar they used such phrases as "republican morality" or "civic virtue," but what they had constantly in mind was the willingness of the good democratic citizen, on critical occasions, to transcend the habitual pursuit of self-interest and devote himself directly and disinterestedly to the common good. In times of war, of course, "republican morality" took the form of patriotism—no one, after all, has ever been able to demonstrate that it is to a man's self-interest to die for his country. In times of peace, "republican morality" might take the form of agreeing to hold public office; since the founding fathers assumed that the holders of such office would be men of property, to whom the pleasures of private life were readily available, and since they further thought of political ambition as a form of human distemper, they could candidly look upon public service as a burden as well as an honor. But whatever the occasion, such a capacity for disinterested action seemed to them—as even today, it still seems to some—a necessary complement to the pursuit of self-interest rightly understood.

Now, given these ideas on how popular government in America could survive and prosper, it is only natural that the founding fathers should have taken a suspicious view of big cities and should have wondered whether, in the end, they could be compatible with a free and popular government. In this suspicion and wonder they were anything but original. The entire literature of classical political philosophy—from Plato, Aristotle, and Cicero on to Montesquieu—exhibits a similar skepticism, to put it mildly, concerning the quality of life that people lead in big cities, and expresses doubt whether the habits of mind generated there—what we might call the urban mentality: irreverent, speculative, pleasure-loving, self-serving, belligerent toward all conventional pieties—are compatible with republican survival. Nor, it should be observed, did the real, historical world present much reassurance, by way of contrary evidence. The big cities that the founding fathers knew or read about all displayed in luxuriant abundance the very vices they wished above all to avoid in the new nation they were constructing. From imperial Rome to imperial London and Paris, the big city was the locus of powerful, illiberal, and undemocratic government, inhabited by people who were either too wretched and depraved to be free, democratic citizens, or by ambitious, self-seeking men to whom the ideals of popular government were utterly alien and even repugnant.

That *small* cities could be soberly and democratically governed, the founding fathers understood well enough—Geneva and Athens and the towns of New England testified to that. That medium-sized cities could sustain a modified and partial form of popular government, based on a deferential citizenry and a patrician elite, they also knew—the histories of republican Rome and Venice were very familiar to them, and their own Boston or Philadelphia offered them living instances of this general truth. But the wisdom of the ages had reached an unequivocal conclusion, in which they concurred, about large, populous, cosmopolitan cities: the anonymous creatures massed in such a place, clawing one another in a sordid scramble for survival, advantage, or specious distinction, their frantic lives reflecting no piety toward nature, God, or the political order—such people were not of the stuff of which a free-standing, self-governing republic could be created. Or, to put this point in a more philosophical way, which would have been immediately comprehensible to our ancestors even if it sounds a little strange to us: if self-government, as an ideal to be respected, means the willingness of people to permit their baser selves to be directed by their better selves, then this precondition of self-government is least likely to be discovered among the turbulent and impassioned masses of big cities.

Today, in the second half of the twentieth century, this theory of the founding fathers is being put to the test, and I do not see how anyone can be blithely sanguine about the ultimate conclusions that will be drawn. Our most obvious difficulty is that we have so many big cities and seem so persistently inept in devising a satisfactory machinery of self-government in them—swinging wildly from the corrupt rule of political machines to abortive experiments in decentralized, direct democracy, with a slovenly bureaucracy providing the barest minimum of stability in between. This is indeed a sore perplexity to us; and no clear solution seems visible even to the most thoughtful among us—witness the uncertainty among our political scientists whether our major cities should evolve into super-cities, almost little states, or whether they would be better off dissolving into mini-cities, almost small towns. Twenty years ago the first prospect seemed the more enchanting; today it is the second; tomorrow the winds of doctrine might once again suddenly reverse themselves. Our ideas about our cities are as unsettled and as uneasy as the cities themselves.

But this obvious difficulty is only the smaller part of the challenge posed us. Though we are indeed becoming ever more "a nation of cities," we are *not*—despite a contrary impression created by the news media—on our way to becoming a nation of very big cities. The proportion of our population in cities of over one million has been drifting downward for several decades now, and this proportion is, in the decades ahead, more likely to decline further than it is to increase. Many of the traditional functions of the great metropolis are being radically decentralized, both by technological and by sociological innovation. Air travel has already robbed the metropolis of its role as a transportation hub for people; air freight is gradually doing the same thing for goods. And just think of the extraordinary way in which our cultural community—our writers and artists and sculptors and musicians and dramatists—has, with recent years, been dispersed among the university campuses of the nation. A city like New York is more and more becoming a showplace for the work of creative artists, rather than a milieu in which they live. Even bohemia, that most urban of cultural phenomena, has been transplanted to and around the university campus.

It is conceivable, therefore, that, though our major cities keep floundering in a sea of troubles, the nation as a whole will not be profoundly affected. And what so many people now proclaim to be an imminent apocalypse may yet turn out to be not much more than—though it is also not much less than— a change of life for our older cities. Even the most critical problem which today confronts these cities—the problem of black Americans living in the squalid isolation of their ghettos —may yet reveal to posterity a very different meaning from the despairing significance we ascribe to it today. For these are the citizens who, if we are lucky, might infuse these cities with a new vigor and a new purpose. It is hard to see who else can accomplish this—it is hard even to see who else would care enough to try. As a white New Yorker, born and bred, I am bound to have confused feelings about such a course of events. But I should like to think I am a sufficiently objective student of the city not to see as a crisis what may merely be a personal problem of adaptation to historical change.

But I digress: because I am a man who has lived all his life in big, old cities, I am inevitably more keenly interested in them than, as a student of the contemporary city, I perhaps ought to be. The overwhelming majority of my fellow Americans clearly prefer to live elsewhere, and this preference is by now an established feature of American life, for better or worse. If we are "a nation of cities," we are also becoming to an ever greater degree a nation of relatively small and middle-sized cities. These are the growing centers of American life—especially if we count as "small cities," as we should, those scattered university campuses which support populations of 30,000 or more. It is quite true that these new cities are not spread uniformly over the land but tend to cluster in what we call "metropolitan areas." This fact has led some observers to conclude hastily that such settlements have only a transient, juridical existence—that they ought properly to be regarded as part of an incipient "megalopolis," in the process of coalescing. This is almost surely an illusion—or, if one prefers, a nightmare. Though a great many urban sociologists and urban journalists seem to be convinced that Americans in large numbers would really prefer to live in the central city and are being forced out of their cities by one external cause or another, the evidence is quite plainly to the contrary. People leave the big cities, or refuse to come to them, because they positively prefer the kinds of lives they can lead in smaller suburban townships or cities of modest size; and these people are not going to become citizens of any kind of "megalopolis."

Indeed, though most central cities are now aware of their ghetto populations only as a source of trouble and calamity, one can predict with considerable confidence that ten years from now these same central cities will be fighting tooth-and-nail to hold on to these populations, as they too begin to experience the attractions of urban life outside our major urban centers.

And here, I think, we have at last come to what I would consider the heart of the matter. For the overwhelming fact of American life today, whether this life be lived in a central city or a suburb or a small city—or even in those rural areas where something like a third of our population still resides—is that it is *life in an urban civilization.* In terms of the *quality* of American life, the United States is now one vast metropolis. Cities are nothing new; the problems of cities are nothing new; but an urban civilization is very new indeed, and the problems of an urban civilization are without precedent in human history.

II

When I say that our urban civilization is something radically new, I am obviously not unmindful of the historical fact that, in a profound sense, just about every civilization we have known has been urban in origin and character. Civilization, both the high and the low of it, is something that has always been bred in cities—which is why all romantic rebels against civilization, in the past as in our own time, so vehemently repudiate the "artificiality" and "superficiality" and "inhumanity" of city life. But the city and its civilization have always been one thing, while the rest of the nation and its way of life have been another. Between these two things there has always existed a high degree of tension—on the whole a creative tension, though it has sometimes found release in exceedingly ugly moments. Between urban life in the city and provincial life outside the city there has always been a gulf of mistrust, suspicion, and contempt. Yet it is not too far-fetched to say that each was an indispensable antibody for the other's healthy existence. Life in the city could, for example, be careless of conventional morality, and even have an experimental attitude toward all moral rules, precisely because of the reassuring certainty that, throughout the rest of the nation, there prevailed a heavy dullness and conformity. This dullness and conformity reassured the city man, even as he mocked it, that his moral experiments were in the nature of singular explorations with no necessary collective consequences. Similarly, the sovereignty of conventional morality outside the city was sustained by reason of the fact that those who would rebel against it simply emigrated to the urban center. In addition, the rigid character of this traditional morality was made more tolerable to the provincial citizenry because of the known and inevitable fact that, in most cases, urban experiments in freedom were not equally or altogether successful for the individual who was presumptuous enough to engage in them. And when they did succeed—when they resulted in artistic creativity or political distinction—the provincial nation participated, at no cost to itself, in the glory.

Now, this provincial nation has been liquidated. To anyone like myself who watches old movies on television—and by old movies I mean no more than fifteen or twenty years old—the most striking impression is of a world that belongs to another era. These movies have farmers' daughters—honest-to-goodness farmers' daughters, with all that this implies for the sophisticated urban imagination; they have happy, neighborly suburban families who smugly and snugly pass the evening watching themselves on television; they have prim schoolmarms and prissy schoolmistresses; they have absent-minded

professors who don't know the difference between a foundation garment and a foundation grant; they have hicks who run
gas stations and cops who drop in for apple pie; they have
children who address their fathers as "sir"; they have virginal
college maidens and hardly any graduate students at all; they
have wildly efficient and fanatically loyal secretaries—in short,
they have a race of people who only yesterday were the
average and the typical, and who have so suddenly become,
in their laughable unreality, a species of "camp."

What has happened, clearly, is that provincial America—that
America which at least paid lip service to, if it did not live by,
the traditional republican morality—that America which,
whether on the farm or in suburb or small town, thought it
important to preserve the appearance of a life lived according
to the prescriptions of an older agrarian virtue and piety—that
America which was calmly philistine and so very, very solid
in its certainties—that America is now part and parcel of urban civilization. The causes of this transformation are so obvious as to need no elaboration; one can simply refer in passing
to the advent of the mass media and of mass higher education,
and there isn't much more that needs to be said. The ultimate
consequences of this transformation, however, are anything
but obvious. We know what happens—both for good and bad;
and it is ineluctably for both good and bad—when an urban
center liberates the energies—both for creation and destruction; and it is ineluctably for both—of provincial emigrés;
what happens constitutes the history of urban civilization. But
we do not know what happens, for the sufficient reason that it
has never happened before, when an urban civilization becomes a mass phenomenon, when the culture of the city becomes everyman's culture, and when urban habits of mind and
modes of living become the common mentality and way of life
for everyone.

If the founding fathers were worried about the effects of a

few large cities upon the American capacity for self-government, what—one wonders—would they make of our new
condition? One is reasonably certain they would regard it as
an utterly impossible state of affairs. And whether they would
be correct in this regard is something that it will be up to us to
determine. Certainly the history of American cities, during
this past century and a half, does not permit us to dismiss their
fears as either irrational or anachronistic. Though these cities
have made America great, and though a city like New York
can be said—especially in these last years, when it has become
a world cultural capital—to have made America glorious, it
does not follow, as we so naturally might think, that they have
strengthened the fundaments of American democracy. Greatness and glory are things the human race has always prized
highly, but we ought not to forget that the political philosophers of democracy have always looked upon them with distrust, as virtues appropriate to empires rather than to self-
governing republics, and have emphasized moral earnestness
and intellectual sobriety as elements that are most wanted in
a democracy.

We can, perhaps, have a better appreciation of the problem
we have created for ourselves if we start from the proposition
—which sounds like a tautology but has far-reaching implications—that in a democracy the people are the ruling class. This
does not mean, of course, that the people as a whole run the
affairs of state or that the people's will finds prompt expression
in the decisions of government. Even in a society which is
officially an aristocracy, the ruling class never has that kind
of instant power and instant authority. Indeed, one suspects
that a government which was *so* responsible would barely have
the capacity to govern at all—and one knows for certain that,
were such a government to exist, it could be manned only by
servile mediocrities who set no value upon their own opinions

or judgment. No, when one says that in a democracy the people are the ruling class, one means that the character of the government and the destiny of the nation are in the longer run determined by the character of the people rather than of any particular class of people.

I know that we are today unaccustomed to thinking in terms such as these, and that the very phrase "the character of the people" has an odd ring to it. In part, this is because American political theory, as it has evolved into American political science, has tended to conceive of democracy exclusively in terms of procedural and mechanical arrangements—in terms of self-interested individuals who rightly understand that it is to their own interest to follow the "rules of the game." This idea goes back to the founding fathers, as has been said—but taken by itself, and divorced from the idea of republican morality, it leads to a self-destructive paradox, as some political scientists have recently come to realize. For when everyone follows the rules of the game, it can then be demonstrated—with all the rigor of a mathematical theorem—that it is to the self-interest of individuals or of organized factions *not* to follow the rules of the game, but simply to take advantage of the fact that the others do. That there are such individuals and factions, only too willing to draw this logical inference, and to act upon it, current American events vividly remind us. And political science, being "value-free," as they say, cannot come up with any persuasive arguments as to why they shouldn't act this way.

Another reason why we cannot seriously contemplate this question of "the character of the people" is that, in the generations which succeeded that of the founding fathers, it came to be believed that this character was not something formed by individual efforts at moral self-definition, but rather that the popular character was inherently good enough—not perfect perhaps, but good enough—so as not to require self-scrutiny. What we may call the transcendental-populist religion of democracy superseded an original political philosophy of democracy. This religion has now so strong a hold that mention of the very idea of a "corrupt people," a common idea in classical political philosophy, is taken as evidence of a nasty antidemocratic bias upon the part of the thinker who would dare entertain it. If things go wrong in our democracy, the persons we are least likely to blame are ourselves. Instead, we seek out the influence of wicked "vested interests," malign "outside agitators," or arrogant "Establishments."

I am not asserting that the American people, at this moment, are a corrupt people—though it worries me that they are so blandly free from self-doubt about this possibility. What I am saying is that they are more and more behaving in a way that would have alarmed the founding fathers even as it would have astonished them. To put it bluntly, they are more and more behaving like a collection of mobs.

III

The term "mob" entered the language in the latter part of the eighteenth century and was used to describe the new populations of the new industrial cities that were then emerging. This population was not only a population uprooted from its villages; it was also *déraciné* with regard to traditional pieties, whether religious, moral, or political. It was a population which felt itself—as in truth it largely was—the victim of external forces, in no way responsible for its own fate, and therefore indifferent to its own character. It was a population which, in its political dependency, could be exploited by unscrupulous profiteers; it was a population which, in its political isolation, could be exploited by zealous demagogues; it was a population which, in its moral bewilderment, could be exploited by wild mystagogues; it was a population whose potential did not go much beyond riotous destructiveness.

It was because the founding fathers did not see how such a population could be capable of self-government that they took so dim a view of large cities. The "mob," as it was then to be seen in London and Paris, and even incipiently in New York or Boston, seemed to them the very antithesis of a democratic citizenry: a citizenry self-reliant, self-determining, and at least firmly touched by, if not thoroughly infused with, republican morality. It takes a transcendental-populist faith of truly enormous dimensions to find in this attitude a mere "agrarian bias." The founding fathers were philosophic men, of no such populist faith, and they had no qualms about insisting that popular government was sustained by "a people" as distinct from a mob.

The history of all modern industrial societies is the story of the gradual transformation of original urban mobs into a people, even as their numbers increased many fold. The secret behind this transformation was not faith but economics—and especially the economics of technological innovation. If it did not occur to the founding fathers that such a transformation was likely or even possible, this was because they could have no intimation of the fantastic economic growth that the coming century and a half would experience. It was not, indeed, until the turn of this century that thinking men began to be shaken loose from their Malthusian spectacles and to be able to see things as they really were. Even so intelligent and liberal a thinker as E. L. Godkin, in several decades of writing for the *Nation*, could not disabuse himself of the notion that the lower urban classes were doomed to exist as something like a permanent mob by the iron laws of Malthusian doctrine. The politics of such a mob, obviously, could only be the politics of expropriation as against the bourgeois politics of participation.

Well, it worked out differently and better. As productivity

increased, the urban mob became an urban citizenry—and, more recently, a suburban citizenry, mimicking in an urban context various aspects of that agrarian life style which was once thought to be of such political significance. The "bourgeois-ification" of society was *the* great event of modern history. Where once we had the bourgeois confronting the masses, we now have bourgeois masses—a fact which has been a source of concern to revolutionary romantics and romantic revolutionaries, both of whom have expectations for the masses which far outrun the bourgeois condition. Even many cautious liberals have been taken aback at the ease with which this society was breeding bourgeois men and women, and a small library of literature was published between 1945 and 1965 that complained of the "homogenization" of American society, of its passionless and conformist quality, of the oppressive weight of consensus, and of the disinclination to conflict and dissent.

That library is now gathering dust, along with the voluminous literature on the iron law of wages. For something very odd and unexpected has, in the past decade, been happening to the bourgeois masses who inhabit our new urban civilization. Though bourgeois in condition and life style, they have become less bourgeois in ethos, and strikingly more mob-like in action. Perhaps this has something to do with a change in the economic character of our bourgeois civilization. Many critics have noted the shift from a producer's ethic (the so-called Protestant ethic) to a consumer's ethic, and go on to affirm that a bourgeois society of widespread affluence is in its essence radically different from a bourgeois society where scarcity automatically imposes a rigorous discipline of its own. This explanation is all the more plausible in that it echoes, in an academic way, the wisdom of the ages as to the corrupting effects of material prosperity upon the social order. The fact that these consequences come as so great a surprise to us—that, having created the kind of affluent society we deliberately aimed at, and having constructed the kind of "progressive" urban civilization we always wanted, that, having done all this, we have also created an unanticipated problem for ourselves —this fact is but a sign of our impoverished political imagination.

The ways in which various strata of our citizenry—from the relatively poor to the relatively affluent—are beginning to behave like a bourgeois urban mob are familiar to anyone who reads his newspaper, and I do not propose to elaborate upon them. The interesting consideration is the extent to which a mob is not simply a physical presence but also, and above everything else, a state of mind. It is, to be precise, that state of mind which lacks all those qualities that, in the opinion of the founding fathers, added up to republican morality: steadiness of character, deliberativeness of mind, and a mild predisposition to subordinate one's own special interests to the public interest. Since the founding fathers could not envisage a nation of bourgeois—a nation of urbanized, prosperous, and strongly acquisitive citizens—they located republican morality in the agrarian sector of American life. We, in this century, have relocated it in the suburban and small-city sector of American life—our contemporary version of America's "grass roots." And it now appears that our anticipations may be treated as roughly by history as were those of the founding fathers.

The causes for this dismaying reversal of expectations are only now being explored by our social critics. Lionel Trilling, especially, has pointed out how the avant-garde, anti-bourgeois, elite culture—what he calls "the adversary culture"—of our bourgeois society has been gradually incorporated into our conventional school curriculum and, with the spread of mass higher education, has begun to shape the popular culture of our urbanized masses. This is an ambiguous process toward which one can only have ambiguous feelings. No one, after all, can sincerely mourn the passing of the *Saturday Evening Post* and of that superficial, provincial, and, above all, philistine popular culture it so smugly affirmed. This culture may have contributed to political stability, but it also represented a spiritual torpor that, in the end, could only be self-defeating because it was so thin in its sense of humanity. On the other hand, there is something positively absurd in the spectacle of prosperous suburban fathers flocking to see—and evidently enjoying—*The Graduate*, or of prosperous, chic, suburban mothers unconcernedly humming "Mrs. Robinson" to themselves as they cheerfully drive off to do their duties as den mothers. This peculiar schizophrenia, suffusing itself through the bourgeois masses of our urban society, may be fun while it lasts; but one may reasonably suppose that, sooner or later, people will decide they would rather not die laughing at themselves, and that some violent convulsions will ensue.

Why the very best art of bourgeois society—the work of our most gifted poets, painters, novelists, and dramatists— should have, and should have had from the very first days of the romantic movement, such an animus against its own bourgeois world is a question one can only speculate on. Presumably it has something to do with the diminished role that disinterested social values, or transcendent religious values, play in a society governed by the principle of self-interest, even perhaps self-interest "rightly understood," but most especially self-interest that makes no effort at self-understanding or self-discipline. But if one can only speculate about the deeper causes of our present disorders, no subtle speculation is needed to see that a democratic-urban civilization which is empty of democratic-urban values is almost surely a civilization in trouble. The symptoms of this trouble plague us every day and in just about every way. If I dwell upon one such symptom, it is only because this one in particular strikes me as so perfectly signifying our inability—it may even be our unwillingness—to comprehend the role of "republican morality" in a democratic-urban civilization. I refer to the problems of drugs.

Now, I have no interest in venturing into the swamp of controversy that surrounds this topic in the conventional terms in which it is publicly discussed. I do not think it so important to ascertain which drugs are medically bad for you, or just how bad each one is. I think the problem of drugs would be just as serious even if it were determined that marijuana, or amphetamines, or LSD were medically harmless; or if some biochemist were to come up with a way to make these drugs—or even a drug like heroin—medically harmless. What makes a drug a truly serious problem is less its medical aspect than its social purpose. Cigarettes are bad for you, but cigarette-smoking poses no kind of threat to our society or to our civilization. Alcohol is likely to cause more harm than good to the average person, but the cocktail party is no threat to our society or our civilization. On the other hand, it is well to recollect that a century ago all social critics agreed that alcohol *was* such a threat, because it was being consumed by the new urban working class in such a way—not only to such a degree, but in such a way—as to demoralize this class and prevent its assimilation into bourgeois, democratic society.

And here we have arrived at the nub of the question as I see it. What counts is *why* drugs or intoxicants are taken, not whether they are. What counts is the meaning and moral status of the action, not its physiological dimensions. Alcohol ceased to be a public issue in this country when social drinking, for purposes of conviviality, succeeded gin-swilling, whose aim was to get out of this world as rapidly as possible. With drugs, the reverse process has taken place. Drug addiction is not itself a new thing; the doctor who would take an occasional shot of morphine so as to be able to keep functioning, the elderly lady who relied upon an opium-laced patent medicine to keep her on her rounds of civic and familial activities—these are familiar enough figures in our past. But today drug-taking has become a mass habit—among our young masses especially —whose purpose is to secede from our society and our civilization; and such a declaration requires a moral answer, not a medical one.

Though the prohibition movement is now very censoriously treated by our American historians, one thing must be said for it: it not only knew the gin mills were medically bad—anyone could see that—it also knew *why* it was bad for a citizen to destroy himself in this way. It had *reasons* to offer, reasons that had to do with the importance of republican morality for those citizens of a self-governing nation—which is to say: the movement for prohibition had a good conscience, both social and moral. Today, in dismal contrast, even those, and they are certainly an overwhelming majority, who believe that the drug habit is bad, seem incapable of giving the reasons why. I mean the real reasons why, which have to do with the reasons why it is desirable to function as an autonomous and self-reliant citizen in our urban, democratic society, rather than to drift through life in a pleasant but enervating haze. The moral code for all civilizations must, at one time or another, be pre-pared to face the ultimate subversive question: "Why not?" Our civilization is now facing that very question in the form of the drug problem, and, apparently, it can only respond with tedious, and in the end ineffectual, medical reports.

It is this startling absence of values that represents the authentic "urban crisis" of our democratic, urban nation. The fact that the word "urbanity" applies both to a condition of urban things and a state of urban mind may be an accident of philology, but if so it is a happy accident, for it reminds us of the interdependence of mind and thing. That same interdependence is to be found in the word "democracy," referring as it does simultaneously to a political system and to the spirit —the idea—that animates this system. The challenge to our urban democracy is to evolve a set of values and a conception of democracy that can function as the equivalent of the "republican morality" of yesteryear. This is our fundamental urban problem. Or, in the immortal words of Pogo: "I have seen the enemy and they is us."

2

The Shaking of the Foundations

EVERY AGE is, in its own way, an "age of anxiety"—the title of a poem by W. H. Auden, written over twenty years ago. Every generation is convinced that its world is out of control, that "things are in the saddle" (Emerson) that "the centre cannot hold" (Yeats), that the past has lost its glory, the present its humanity, the future its hope. The premonition of apocalypse springs eternal in the human breast.

It is comforting to reflect that for most of humanity none of these premonitions is ever justified: the Day of the Beast has yet to dawn. Somehow, the human race endures, life continues to yield its modest satisfactions; the world doesn't actually come to an end.

It is less comforting but more realistic to reflect that we don't live in *the* world; we live in a particular world; and history records many particular worlds that did indeed come to their ends—sometimes abruptly, more often slowly and insensibly, but always painfully for those who felt themselves to be part of what was being destroyed. And today one does have cause to believe that we are approaching one of those historic watersheds that separate worlds in time.

Who can deny that, in the United States today, as never before in its history, there is a vast unease about the prospects of the republic? It is an unease all the more unsettling in that it is so hard to define. We know the problems of American society—know them with an unparalleled scholarship and an incomparable attentiveness. None of these problems, taken by itself, seems insoluble. But taken together, they constitute a condition and are creating habits of mind that threaten the civic-bourgeois culture bequeathed to us by Western civilization.

That last phrase is vague, as it must be, covering as it does some four centuries of history, more than a dozen nations, and a great variety of cultural modes. Still, the phrase is not meaningless. It does refer to a social order and a way of life in which the adult population is presumed to be composed of rational, free, and responsible *citizens*—that very word is itself a kind of key, for the citizen is something different from the subject of a regime, or the member of a movement, or the adherent of a creed. And one gets the distinct impression, surveying the world around us, that citizens are, to an increasing degree, in short supply.

What makes the situation all the more ominous is that the civic-bourgeois culture is not being overwhelmed from without, but is rather being casually and almost contemptuously subverted from within. Those subverting it are hard to identify, since almost all of us have something of a hand in it, at one moment or another. Neither the radical left nor the radical right has been notably successful in creating viable alternatives to liberal democracy, and there has been no massive doctrinal conversion to new orthodoxies. (Indeed, it is where there are totalitarian regimes that the bourgeois-civic values seem most alive in the populace—where people seem to want desperately to become citizens.) Rather, what is happening is something that is both less obvious and more unsettling. It involves the slow draining away of legitimacy from existing institutions and prevailing traditions.

Over the entire world, there is scarcely an institution whose legitimacy is not suddenly liable to peremptory challenge. It doesn't appear to matter whether the institution is working well or not: ten years ago most people thought American universities were working better than ever. And it doesn't seem to matter whether people are materially well off or not: the French workers are far better off than they were a decade ago. What exists is vulnerable for no other reason than that it exists—and because the citizenry no longer feels any particular responsibility for its existence, any instinctive obligation to sustain or even reform it.

The effect is of disengagement and a sense of powerlessness on the part of the majority, of alienation and irresponsible power on the part of every organized minority, and of purposelessness on the part of both. "What do people want?" the politicians wonder, just as confusedly as the rest of us. And when they or we think an answer is at hand, it doesn't stand up for long. Today's solution is tomorrow's dilemma. We study the future more furiously than ever before, so as to be prepared for eventualities. But it is as instructive as it is humiliating to note that no sociologist, in the 1950's, predicted that the movement for civil rights would give rise to black nationalism in this country, and that no educational leader foresaw the way in which the expansion of educational opportunity would give birth to a revolt on the campus. It's bad enough when things are in the saddle; it's worse when we can't even identify the bloody horse.

It is likely that, a century or two from now, students taking exams will be asked to list the causes of this period's unrest and to describe how contemporaries viewed the process. No doubt it will turn out that those contemporaries—i.e., we—had only a dim and imperfect comprehension of what was happening to them. Still, we must understand as best we can; and it seems to me that there are five major experiences we are living through that are mainly responsible for those shivers of foreboding now diffused throughout our body politic.

• *The Technological Imperative:* There is a widespread conviction among Americans that the growth of scientific knowledge and the speed of technological innovation have now achieved such self-determined momentum as to make ours "the accidental century" and "the temporary society"—to quote the titles of two recent books. Oddly enough, it is not at all clear that this conviction can be validly inferred from the facts of the case. There really is very little statistical evidence that technological innovation—or the diffusion of technological innovation—today proceeds at a pace significantly faster than that of two or three or five decades ago. Nor is there convincing evidence that men's personal lives are being directly affected by technology to a degree and extent unknown by previous generations. Most of us live in homes, work at jobs, and play at games that are not radically different from those of our parents. But a *feeling* of radical difference does exist—and feelings are every bit as real as social statistics.

Besides, it is possible that this feeling expresses a truth that escapes mere statistics. Thus, it may be—as some claim—that technology really is on the verge of drastically changing our lives; that the popular sentiment is caused by a vaguely envisaged future rather than an experienced past or present. The *possibilities* of our future, at least, are quite different from those envisaged by our parents. In our case, the scientific possibilities include wiping out the human race, space travel into unimaginable universes, breeding human beings to specification, and much else besides. To be even dimly aware of these possibilities is to have one's vision of what is "natural" quite shattered.

Furthermore, even the direct changes already imposed on our lives by new technology, unsensational as they mostly are, may be having a delayed effect on us. Just as a steady, high speed in a car *over a long period of time* may induce feelings of nausea and vertigo, the effects of a dynamic society may be cumulative in a way that we cannot easily explain.

Whatever the explanation, however, it is beyond question that Americans do have the sensation that the worlds of science fiction are beginning to pervade, in a strange and threatening way, the familiar, bourgeois American world they have known and loved. And they have the further, queasy sensation that there is nothing anyone can do about it.

• *The Revolution of Rising Expectations:* There is nothing more frustrating than to expect the impossible as a matter of right, and yet such expectations are by now second nature to a large part of humanity. To see something on television is to feel entitled to it; to be promised something by a politician is to feel immediately deprived of it. What is called "the revolution of rising expectations" has reached such grotesque dimensions that men take it as an insult when they are asked to be reasonable in their desires and demands. The reasonable is what they expect to obtain automatically. The unreasonable is what they look to government to provide by special, ingenious effort. And, through its own credulity, or its cynicism, or both, modern government does feel compelled to promise not only the effort but the success of this effort.

But when people are determinedly unreasonable, all promises eventually fail and coercion of one kind or another is inevitable. In nation after nation such coercion is being desperately relied upon. Because the United States is so rich and productive, our society has so far been able, far better than any other, to placate the "revolution of rising expectations." Nevertheless, there is a mounting irritability, impatience, distemper, and mistrust. Each individual and every organized group (racial, economic, professional, etc.), seeing no justification for self-discipline—indeed, holding the very idea of self-discipline in a kind of contempt—calls for ever greater discipline to be exercised against the rest. Self-government, the basic principle of this republic, is inexorably being eroded in favor of self-seeking, self-indulgence, and just plain aggressive selfishness. This may be an inevitable consequence of "affluence," with its emphasis on material goods. It may be an inevitable consequence of democracy, with its egalitarian dynamic. But it is what is happening. Already an entire generation exists which simply cannot believe that American school textbooks used to extol "self-denial" as a virtue.

• *The Generation Gap:* In every dynamic society there is always a generation gap, for in a changing world the young will always have different habits, viewpoints, and styles from the old. But in the 1960's the gap opened to a point where the very fabric of our society threatens to be rent altogether. As with technology, it may well be that nothing "new" is happening, merely that cumulative tensions of decades are beginning to find ultimate expression. Still, the effect is to all intents and purposes the same. The young not only live in a world of their own—they have always done that, more or less. They now live—an increasing number now live—in an *anti*-world, one whose existence challenges the legitimacy of the adult world.

The turmoil on our campuses is the most obvious sign of these worlds in collision. Any sensible adult knows that young people can be—and there are always some who will be—rebellious, wayward, defiant, dissenting. That youth should desire to see the world different from what it is, should incorporate into their own life styles this desire and this difference, is not an unfamiliar idea. What *is* unfamiliar is the idea that youth may properly engage in a serious struggle for power against their parents and elders. Young people have always resisted or evaded the moral authority of their parents, on the assumption that it was out of date. But never before has the right of adults to any moral authority whatsoever been challenged.

• *Our Changing Popular Culture:* For more than a century now, there has prevailed a condition of hostility between the high culture of the Western world and the bourgeois society it inhabited. This culture has largely been contemptuous of capitalism, liberalism, democracy, materialism, organized religion, and all the familiar domestic virtues. As to why this is so, one can speculate endlessly: in the end, it may simply be that artists find a highly civil society less congenial to their imaginations than a heroic and adventurous one. But whatever the reason, it remains true that a great preponderance of the important poets and novelists and painters in the modern tradition have been hostile to this world, regardless of whether or not this world was hostile to them.

So long as the "adversary culture" was restricted to an avant-garde elite, the social and political consequences of this state of affairs were minimal. (The aesthetic consequences were, paradoxically, enormously fruitful: the anti-bourgeois arts represent one of the great achievements of bourgeois civilization.) The prevailing popular culture, however artistically deficient, accepted the moral and social conventions—or deviated from them in conventionally accepted ways. But in the 1960's the avant-garde culture made a successful take-over bid, so to speak, and has now become our popular culture as well. Perhaps this is, once again, simply the cumulative impact of a long process; perhaps—almost surely—it has something to do with the tremendous expansion of higher education in our times. In any case, it has unambiguously happened: the most "daring" and self-styled "subversive" or "pornographic" texts of modern literature, once the precious possession of a happy few, are now read as a matter of course—are read in required courses—by youngsters in junior colleges all over the country. The avant-garde has become a popular cultural militia. Hollywood is already a conquered province: neither *Bonnie and Clyde* nor *The Graduate* could have been pro-duced—or, if produced, distributed—a mere ten years ago. Television still holds out, but it surely cannot continue to for long.

One wonders: how can a bourgeois society survive in a cul-tural ambiance that derides every traditional bourgeois virtue and celebrates promiscuity, homosexuality, drugs, political terrorism—anything, in short, that is in bourgeois eyes per-verse? Publicly, we are all tolerant of these new cultural modes, in part because we fear not to be "with it," partly be-cause they often are intrinsically illuminating. But beneath this surface tolerance there lie depths of anxiety. Our world is being emptied of its ideal content, and the imposing institu-tional façade sways in the wind.

 • *The Decline of Religion:* This is the most profound change of all—so profound that it is hard to ascribe any single conse-quence directly to it, since in one way or another everything is connected with it.

All human societies have to respond to two fundamental questions. The first is: "Why?" The second is: "Why not?" *Why* behave in such and such a way? *Why not* behave differ-ently or contrarily? A liberal society can rely on a more or less persuasive, as against an explicitly authoritative, answer to the first question. But no society can endure speechless before the second.

It is religion that, traditionally, has supplied the answers to these questions. In our ever more secularized society, it is still religion that has supplied the answer to the second. Today, it cannot do so: the "why nots" are being insistently asked within the organized churches themselves. Call it "the Death of God," or "Situation Ethics," or what you will, the fact remains that religious thinkers today are anxiously posing the very same crucial question we have always looked to religion to answer. This may be theologically exciting; it is also humanly and socially disorienting. The upshot is that—as Professor Earl Rovit recently observed—on an ever larger scale "why not" is ceasing to be a question at all. It is becoming a kind of answer.

Decline of Religion

Why? Why not? } All societies have to respond to + fundamental problems!

Why behave in a particular way?

Why not behave differently or contrarily?

Religion traditionally answered these questions. It is still religion that answers "Why not?"

* Today churches are asking also asking "why not?"
Ex. Sit. Ethics, Death of God

* Today, "why not" is ceasing to be a question at all. It is becoming a kind of answer. Prob. Zane Rorit?

3

Pornography, Obscenity,
and the Case for Censorship

BEING FRUSTRATED is disagreeable, but the real dis-
asters in life begin when you get what you want. For almost
a century now, a great many intelligent, well-meaning and articulate people—of a kind generally called liberal or intellectual, or both—have argued eloquently against any kind of censorship of art and/or entertainment. And within the past ten
years, the courts and the legislatures of most Western nations
have found these arguments persuasive—so persuasive that
hardly a man is now alive who clearly remembers what the
answers to these arguments were. Today, in the United States
and other democracies, censorship has to all intents and purposes ceased to exist.

Is there a sense of triumphant exhilaration in the land?
Hardly. There is, on the contrary, a rapidly growing unease
and disquiet. Somehow, things have not worked out as they
were supposed to, and many notable civil libertarians have
gone on record as saying this was not what they meant at all.
They wanted a world in which *Desire Under the Elms* could
be produced, or *Ulysses* published, without interference by

philistine busybodies holding public office. They have got that, of course; but they have also got a world in which homosexual rape takes place on the stage, in which the public flocks during lunch hours to witness varieties of professional fornication, in which Times Square has become little more than a hideous market for the sale and distribution of printed filth that panders to all known (and some fanciful) sexual perversions.

But disagreeable as this may be, does it really matter? Might not our unease and disquiet be merely a cultural hangover—a "hangup," as they say? What reason is there to think that anyone was ever corrupted by a book?

This last question, oddly enough, is asked by the very same people who seem convinced that advertisements in magazines or displays of violence on television do indeed have the power to corrupt. It is also asked, incredibly enough and in all sincerity, by people—e.g., university professors and schoolteachers—whose very lives provide all the answers one could want. After all, if you believe that no one was ever corrupted by a book, you have also to believe that no one was ever improved by a book (or a play or a movie). You have to believe, in other words, that all art is morally trivial and that, consequently, all education is morally irrelevant. No one, not even a university professor, really believes that.

To be sure, it is extremely difficult, as social scientists tell us, to trace the effects of any single book (or play or movie) on an individual reader or any class of readers. But we all know, and social scientists know it too, that the ways in which we use our minds and imaginations do shape our characters and help define us as persons. That those who certainly know this are nevertheless moved to deny it merely indicates how a dogmatic resistance to the idea of censorship can—like most dogmatism—result in a mindless insistence on the absurd.

I have used these harsh terms—"dogmatism" and "mindless"

—advisedly. I might also have added "hypocritical." For the plain fact is that none of us is a complete civil libertarian. We all believe that there is some point at which the public authorities ought to step in to limit the "self expression" of an individual or a group, even where this might be seriously intended as a form of artistic expression, and even where the artistic transaction is between consenting adults. A playwright or theatrical director might, in this crazy world of ours, find someone willing to commit suicide on the stage, as called for by the script. We would not allow that—any more than we would permit scenes of real physical torture on the stage, even if the victim were a willing masochist. And I know of no one, no matter how free in spirit, who argues that we ought to permit gladiatorial contests in Yankee Stadium, similar to those once performed in the Colosseum at Rome—even if only consenting adults were involved.

The basic point that emerges is one that Prof. Walter Berns has powerfully argued: no society can be utterly indifferent to the ways its citizens publicly entertain themselves.* Bear-baiting and cockfighting are prohibited only in part out of compassion for the suffering animals; the main reason they were abolished was because it was felt that they debased and brutalized the citizenry who flocked to witness such spectacles. And the question we face with regard to pornography and obscenity is whether, now that they have such strong legal protection from the Supreme Court, they can or will brutalize and debase our citizenry. We are, after all, not dealing with one passing incident—one book, or one play, or one movie. We are dealing with a general tendency that is suffusing our entire culture.

I say pornography *and* obscenity because, though they have different dictionary definitions and are frequently distinguish-

* This is as good a place as any to express my profound indebtedness to Walter's Berns's superb essay, "Pornography vs. Democracy," in the winter, 1971 issue of *The Public Interest*.

able as "artistic" genres, they are nevertheless in the end identical in effect. Pornography is not objectionable simply because it arouses sexual desire or lust or prurience in the mind of the reader or spectator; this is a silly Victorian notion. A great many nonpornographic works—including some parts of the Bible—excite sexual desire very successfully. What is distinctive about pornography is that, in the words of D. H. Lawrence, it attempts "to do dirt on [sex] . . . [It is an] insult to a vital human relationship."

In other words, pornography differs from erotic art in that its whole purpose is to treat human beings obscenely, to deprive human beings of their specifically human dimension. That is what obscenity is all about. It is light years removed from any kind of carefree sensuality—there is no continuum between Fielding's *Tom Jones* and the Marquis de Sade's *Justine*. These works have quite opposite intentions. To quote Susan Sontag: "What pornographic literature does is precisely to drive a wedge between one's existence as a full human being and one's existence as a sexual being—while in ordinary life a healthy person is one who prevents such a gap from opening up." This definition occurs in an essay *defending* pornography—Miss Sontag is a candid as well as gifted critic —so the definition, which I accept, is neither tendentious nor censorious.

Along these same lines, one can point out—as C. S. Lewis pointed out some years back—that it is no accident that in the history of all literatures obscene words, the so-called "four-letter words," have always been the vocabulary of farce or vituperation. The reason is clear; they reduce men and women to some of their mere bodily functions—they reduce man to his animal component, and such a reduction is an essential purpose of farce or vituperation.

Similarly, Lewis also suggested that it is not an accident that we have no offhand, colloquial, neutral terms—not in any

Western European language at any rate—for our most private parts. The words we do use are either (a) nursery terms, (b) archaisms, (c) scientific terms, or (d) a term from the gutter (i.e., a demeaning term). Here I think the genius of language is telling us something important about man. It is telling us that man is an animal with a difference: he has a unique sense of privacy, and a unique capacity for shame when this privacy is violated. Our "private parts" are indeed private, and not merely because convention prescribes it. This particular convention is indigenous to the human race. In practically all primitive tribes, men and women cover their private parts; and in practically all primitive tribes, men and women do not copulate in public.

It may well be that Western society, in the latter half of the twentieth century, is experiencing a drastic change in sexual mores and sexual relationships. We have had many such "sexual revolutions" in the past—the bourgeois family and bourgeois ideas of sexual propriety were themselves established in the course of a revolution against eighteenth-century "licentiousness"—and we shall doubtless have others in the future. It is, however, highly improbable (to put it mildly) that what we are witnessing is the Final Revolution which will make sexual relations utterly unproblematic, permit us to dispense with any kind of ordered relationships between the sexes, and allow us freely to redefine the human condition. And so long as humanity has not reached that utopia, obscenity will remain a problem.

II

One of the reasons it will remain a problem is that obscenity is not merely about sex, any more than science fiction is about science. Science fiction, as every student of the genre knows, is a peculiar vision of power: what it is really about is politics.

And obscenity is a peculiar vision of humanity: what it is really about is ethics and metaphysics.

Imagine a man—a well-known man, much in the public eye —in a hospital ward, dying an agonizing death. He is not in control of his bodily functions, so that his bladder and his bowels empty themselves of their own accord. His consciousness is overwhelmed and extinguished by pain, so that he cannot communicate with us, nor we with him. Now, it would be, technically, the easiest thing in the world to put a television camera in his hospital room and let the whole world witness this spectacle. We don't do it—at least we don't do it as yet— because we regard this as an *obscene* invasion of privacy. And what would make the spectacle obscene is that we would be witnessing the extinguishing of humanity in a human animal.

Incidentally, in the past our humanitarian crusaders against capital punishment understood this point very well. The abolitionist literature goes into great physical detail about what happens to a man when he is hanged or electrocuted or gassed. And their argument was—and is—that what happens is shockingly obscene, and that no civilized society should be responsible for perpetrating such obscenities, particularly since in the nature of the case there must be spectators to ascertain that this horror was indeed being perpetrated in fulfillment of the law.

Sex—like death—is an activity that is both animal and human. There are human sentiments and human ideals involved in this animal activity. But when sex is public, the viewer does not see—cannot see—the sentiments and the ideals. He can only see the animal coupling. And that is why, when men and women make love, as we say, they prefer to be alone—because it is only when you are alone that you can make love, as distinct from merely copulating in an animal and casual way. And that, too, is why those who are voyeurs, if they are not

irredeemably sick, also feel ashamed at what they are witnessing. When sex is a public spectacle, a human relationship has
been debased into a mere animal connection.

It is also worth noting that this making of sex into an obscenity is not a mutual and equal transaction but rather an act
of exploitation by one of the partners—the male partner. I do
not wish to get into the complicated question as to what, if
any, are the essential differences—as distinct from conventional
and cultural differences—between male and female. I do not
claim to know the answer to that. But I do know—and I take
it as a sign that has meaning—that pornography is, and always
has been, a man's work; that women rarely write pornography;
and that women tend to be indifferent consumers of pornography.* My own guess, by way of explanation, is that a
woman's sexual experience is ordinarily more suffused with
human emotion than is man's, that men are more easily satisfied with autoerotic activities, and that men can therefore more
easily take a more "technocratic" view of sex and its pleasures.
Perhaps this is not correct. But whatever the explanation, there
can be no question that pornography is a form of "sexism,"
as the women's liberation movement calls it, and that the instinct of women's liberation has been unerring in perceiving
that when pornography is perpetrated, it is perpetrated against
them, as part of a conspiracy to deprive them of their full
humanity.

But even if all this is granted, it might be said—and doubtless
will be said—that I really ought not to be unduly concerned.
Free competition in the cultural marketplace—it is argued
by people who have never otherwise had a kind word to say
for laissez-faire—will automatically dispose of the problem.

* There are, of course, a few exceptions. *L'Histoire d'O*, for instance, was
written by a woman. It is unquestionably the most *melancholy* work of
pornography ever written. And its theme is precisely the dehumanization
accomplished by obscenity.

The present fad for pornography and obscenity, it will be asserted, is just that, a fad. It will spend itself in the course of time; people will get bored with it, will be able to take it or leave it alone in a casual way, in a "mature way," and, in sum, I am being unnecessarily distressed about the whole business. *The New York Times*, in an editorial, concludes hopefully in this vein.

In the end . . . the insensate pursuit of the urge to shock, carried from one excess to a more abysmal one, is bound to achieve its own antidote in total boredom. When there is no lower depth to descend to, ennui will erase the problem.

I would like to be able to go along with this line of reasoning, but I cannot. I think it is false, and for two reasons, the first psychological, the second political.

The basic psychological fact about pornography and obscenity is that it appeals to and provokes a kind of sexual regression. The sexual pleasure one gets from pornography and obscenity is autoerotic and infantile; put bluntly, it is a masturbatory exercise of the imagination, when it is not masturbation pure and simple. Now, people who masturbate do not get bored with masturbation, just as sadists don't get bored with sadism, and voyeurs don't get bored with voyeurism.

In other words, infantile sexuality is not only a permanent temptation for the adolescent or even the adult—it can quite easily become a permanent, self-reinforcing neurosis. It is because of an awareness of this possibility of regression toward the infantile condition, a regression which is always open to us, that all the codes of sexual conduct ever devised by the human race take such a dim view of autoerotic activities and try to discourage autoerotic fantasies. Masturbation is indeed a perfectly natural autoerotic activity, as so many sexologists blandly assure us today. And it is precisely because it is so perfectly natural that it can be so dangerous to the mature or maturing person, if it is not controlled or sublimated in some way. That is the true meaning of Portnoy's complaint. Portnoy, you will recall, grows up to be a man who is incapable of having an adult sexual relationship with a woman; his sexuality remains fixed in an infantile mode, the prisoner of his autoerotic fantasies. Inevitably, Portnoy comes to think, in a perfectly *infantile* way, that it was all his mother's fault.

It is true that, in our time, some quite brilliant minds have come to the conclusion that a reversion to infantile sexuality is the ultimate mission and secret destiny of the human race. I am thinking in particular of Norman O. Brown, for whose writings I have the deepest respect. One of the reasons I respect them so deeply is that Mr. Brown is a serious thinker who is unafraid to face up to the radical consequences of his radical theories. Thus, Mr. Brown knows and says that for his kind of salvation to be achieved, humanity must annul the civilization it has created—not merely the civilization we have today, but all civilization—so as to be able to make the long descent backward into animal innocence.

And that is the point. What is at stake is civilization and humanity, nothing less. The idea that "everything is permitted," as Nietzsche put it, rests on the premise of nihilism and has nihilistic implications. I will not pretend that the case against nihilism and for civilization is an easy one to make. We are here confronting the most fundamental of philosophical questions, on the deepest levels. In short, the matter of pornography and obscenity is not a trivial one, and only superficial minds can take a bland and untroubled view of it.

In this connection, I must also point out those who are primarily against censorship on liberal grounds tell us not to take pornography or obscenity seriously, while those who are for pornography and obscenity on radical grounds take it very seriously indeed. I believe the radicals—writers like Susan Sontag, Herbert Marcuse, Norman O. Brown, and even Jerry Rubin—are right, and the liberals are wrong. I also believe that those young radicals at Berkeley, some seven years ago, who provoked a major confrontation over the public use of obscene words, showed a brilliant political instinct. And once Mark Rudd could publicly ascribe to the president of Columbia a notoriously obscene relationship to his mother, without provoking any kind of reaction, the S.D.S. had already won the day. The occupation of Columbia's buildings merely ratified their victory. Men who show themselves unwilling to defend civilization against nihilism are not going to be either resolute or effective in defending the university against anything.

III

I am already touching upon a political aspect of pornography when I suggest that it is inherently and purposefully subversive of civilization and its institutions. But there is another and more specifically political aspect, which has to do with the relationship of pornography and/or obscenity to democracy, and especially to the quality of public life on which democratic government ultimately rests.

Though the phrase "the quality of life" trips easily from so many lips these days, it tends to be one of those clichés with many trivial meanings and no large, serious one. Sometimes it merely refers to such externals as the enjoyment of cleaner air, cleaner water, cleaner streets. At other times it refers to the merely private enjoyment of music, painting, or literature. Rarely does it have anything to do with the way the citizen in a democracy views himself—his obligations, his intentions, his ultimate self-definition.

Instead, what I would call the "managerial" conception of democracy is the predominant opinion among political scientists, sociologists, and economists, and has, through the untiring efforts of these scholars, become the conventional journalistic opinion as well. The root idea behind this "managerial" conception is that democracy is a "political system" (as they say) which can be adequately defined in terms of—can be fully reduced to—its mechanical arrangements. Democracy is then seen as a set of rules and procedures, and *nothing but* a set of rules and procedures, whereby majority rule and minority rights are reconciled into a state of equilibrium. If everyone follows these rules and procedures, then a democracy is in working order. I think this is a fair description of the democratic idea that currently prevails in academia. One can also fairly say that it is now the liberal idea of democracy par excellence.

I cannot help but feel that there is something ridiculous about being this kind of a democrat, and I must further confess to having a sneaking sympathy for those of our young radicals who also find it ridiculous. The absurdity is the absurdity of idolatry—of taking the symbolic for the real, the means for the end. The purpose of democracy cannot possibly be the endless functioning of its own political machinery. The purpose of any political regime is to achieve some version of the good life and the good society. It is not at all difficult to imagine a perfectly functioning democracy which answers all questions except one—namely, why should anyone of intelligence and spirit care a fig for it?

There is, however, an older idea of democracy—one which was fairly common until about the beginning of this century —for which the conception of the quality of public life is absolutely crucial. This idea starts from the proposition that democracy is a form of self-government, and that if you want it to be a meritorious polity, you have to care about what kind of people govern it. Indeed, it puts the matter more strongly and declares that if you want self-government, you are only entitled to it if that "self" is worthy of governing. There is no inherent right to self-government if it means that such government is vicious, mean, squalid, and debased. Only a dogmatist and a fanatic, an idolater of democratic machinery, could approve of self-government under such conditions.

And because the desirability of self-government depends on the character of the people who govern, the older idea of democracy was very solicitous of the condition of this character. It was solicitous of the individual self, and felt an obligation to educate it into what used to be called "republican virtue." And it was solicitous of that collective self which we call public opinion and which, in a democracy, governs us collectively. Perhaps in some respects it was nervously oversolicitous —that would not be surprising. But the main thing is that it cared, cared not merely about the machinery of democracy but about the quality of life that this machinery might generate.

And because it cared, this older idea of democracy had no problem in principle with pornography and/or obscenity. It censored them—and it did so with a perfect clarity of mind and a perfectly clear conscience. It was not about to permit people capriciously to corrupt themselves. Or, to put it more precisely: in this version of democracy, the people took some care not to let themselves be governed by the more infantile and irrational parts of themselves.

I have, it may be noticed, uttered that dreadful word "censorship." And I am not about to back away from it. If you think pornography and/or obscenity is a serious problem, you have to be for censorship. I'll go even further and say that if you want to prevent pornography and/or obscenity from becoming a problem, you have to be for censorship. And lest there be any misunderstanding as to what I am saying, I'll put it as bluntly as possible: if you care for the quality of life in our American democracy, then you have to be for censorship.

IV

But can a liberal be for censorship? Unless one assumes that being a liberal *must* mean being indifferent to the quality of American life, then the answer has to be: yes, a liberal can be for censorship—but he ought to favor a liberal form of censorship.

Is that a contradiction in terms? I don't think so. We have no problem in contrasting *repressive* laws governing alcohol and drugs and tobacco with laws *regulating* (i.e., discouraging the sale of) alcohol and drugs and tobacco. Laws encouraging temperance are not the same thing as laws that have as their goal prohibition or abolition. We have not made the smoking of cigarettes a criminal offense. We have, however, and with good liberal conscience, prohibited cigarette advertising on television, and may yet, again with good liberal conscience, prohibit it in newspapers and magazines. The idea of restricting individual freedom, in a liberal way, is not at all unfamiliar to us.

I therefore see no reason why we should not be able to distinguish repressive censorship from liberal censorship of the written and spoken word. In Britain, until a few years ago, you could perform almost any play you wished, but certain plays, judged to be obscene, had to be performed in private theatrical clubs which were deemed to have a "serious" interest in theater. In the United States, all of us who grew up using public libraries are familiar with the circumstances under which certain books could be circulated only to adults, while still other books had to be read in the library reading room, under the librarian's skeptical eye. In both cases, a small minority that was willing to make a serious effort to see an obscene play or read an obscene book could do so. But the impact of obscenity was circumscribed and the quality of public life was only marginally affected.*

I am not saying it is easy in practice to sustain a distinction between liberal and repressive censorship, especially in the public realm of a democracy, where popular opinion is so vulnerable to demagoguery. Moreover, an acceptable system of liberal censorship is likely to be exceedingly difficult to devise in the United States today, because our educated classes, upon whose judgment a liberal censorship must rest, are so convinced that there is no such thing as a problem of obscenity, or even that there is no such thing as obscenity at all. But, to counterbalance this, there is the further, fortunate truth that the tolerable margin for error is quite large, and single mistakes or single injustices are not all that important.

This possibility of error, of course, occasions much distress among artists and academics. It is a fact, one that cannot and should not be denied, that any system of censorship is bound, upon occasion, to treat unjustly a particular work of art—to find pornography where there is only gentle eroticism, to find obscenity where none really exists, or to find both where its existence ought to be tolerated because it serves a larger moral purpose. Though most works of art are not obscene, and though most obscenity has nothing to do with art, there are some few works of art that are, at least in part, pornographic and/or obscene. There are also some few works of art that are

---

* It is fairly predictable that someone is going to object that this point of view is "elitist"—that, under a system of liberal censorship, the rich will have privileged access to pornography and obscenity. Yes, of course, they will—just as, at present, the rich have privileged access to heroin if they want it. But one would have to be an egalitarian maniac to object to this state of affairs on the grounds of equality.

in the special category of the comic-ironic "bawdy" (Boccaccio, Rabelais). It is such works of art that are likely to suffer at the hands of the censor. That is the price one has to be prepared to pay for censorship—even liberal censorship.

But just how high is this price? If you believe, as so many artists seem to believe today, that art is the only sacrosanct activity in our profane and vulgar world—that any man who designates himself an artist thereby acquires a sacred office —then obviously censorship is an intolerable form of sacrilege. But for those of us who do not subscribe to this religion of art, the costs of censorship do not seem so high at all.

If you look at the history of American or English literature, there is precious little damage you can point to as a consequence of the censorship that prevailed throughout most of that history. Very few works of literature—of real literary merit, I mean—ever were suppressed; and those that were, were not suppressed for long. Nor have I noticed, now that censorship of the written word has to all intents and purposes ceased in this country, that hitherto suppressed or repressed masterpieces are flooding the market. Yes, we can now read *Fanny Hill* and the Marquis de Sade. Or, to be more exact, we can now openly purchase them, since many people were able to read them even though they were publicly banned, which is as it should be under a liberal censorship. So how much have literature and the arts gained from the fact that we can all now buy them over the counter, that, indeed, we are all now encouraged to buy them over the counter? They have not gained much that I can see.

And one might also ask a question that is almost never raised: how much has literature lost from the fact that everything is now permitted? It has lost quite a bit, I should say. In a free market, Gresham's Law can work for books or theater as efficiently as it does for coinage—driving out the good, establishing the debased. The cultural market in the United States today is being pre-empted by dirty books, dirty movies, dirty theater. A pornographic novel has a far better chance of being published today than a nonpornographic one, and quite a few pretty good novels are not being published at all simply because they are not pornographic, and are therefore less likely to sell. Our cultural condition has not improved as a result of the new freedom. American cultural life wasn't much to brag about twenty years ago; today one feels ashamed for it.

Just one last point which I dare not leave untouched. If we start censoring pornography or obscenity, shall we not inevitably end up censoring political opinion? A lot of people seem to think this would be the case—which only shows the power of doctrinaire thinking over reality. We had censorship of pornography and obscenity for 150 years, until almost yesterday, and I am not aware that freedom of opinion in this country was in any way diminished as a consequence of this fact. Fortunately for those of us who are liberal, freedom is not indivisible. If it were, the case for liberalism would be indistinguishable from the case for anarchy; and they are two very different things.

But I must repeat and emphasize: what kind of laws we pass governing pornography and obscenity, what kind of censorship—or, since we are still a federal nation, what kinds of censorship—we institute in our various localities may indeed be difficult matters to cope with; nevertheless the real issue is one of principle. I myself subscribe to a liberal view of the enforcement problem: I think that pornography should be illegal *and* available to anyone who wants it so badly as to make a pretty strenuous effort to get it. We have lived with under-the-counter pornography for centuries now, in a fairly comfortable way. But the issue of principle, of whether it should be over or under the counter, has to be settled before we can reflect on the advantages and disadvantages of alternative modes of censorship. I think the settlement we are living under now, in which obscenity and democracy are regarded as equals, is wrong; I believe it is inherently unstable; I think it will, in the long run, be incompatible with any authentic concern for the quality of life in our democracy.

4

American Historians and
the Democratic Idea

ALTHOUGH IT IS HARDLY A SECRET, I had better affirm
it explicitly right at the outset: I am no kind of historian. I am a
journalist, at best a man of letters, and I am keenly aware that,
as Voltaire observed, a man of letters resembles a flying fish:
"If he raises himself up a little, the birds devour him; if he
dives, the fish eat him up." I take this to mean that insofar as I
refer to general ideas, I shall be devoured by the scholarly
eagles, and that insofar as I refer to particular details, I shall
be eaten alive by the scholarly sharks. On the other hand, it is
in the nature of a flying fish that he cannot for too long skim
nervously along the surface. That suits neither his instincts
nor his appetite. So, in what follows, I shall be at the historian's mercy, without really expecting any from him.

As a matter of fact the only reason I feel justified in propos-
ing these thoughts to a scholarly public is that some years ago
I set out to write a book. The book was supposed to deal with
the present state of the democratic idea in America and with

A paper read to the annual conference of the Organization of American
Historians at Philadelphia, April, 1969.

the way in which the ambiguities surrounding this idea have been the cause of many of our contemporary social and political problems. For obvious reasons, some background reading in American history seemed like a useful preparatory exercise. Well, that exercise turned out to be more strenuous and less satisfying than I anticipated. To my dismay, I discovered that, far from providing me with any convenient, ready-made historical perspective on the fate of the democratic idea in America, most American historians simply offered me further and quite unwelcome evidence of, first, how confused this idea has been during most of America's history and, second, how confused American historians themselves have been about this idea. It is not that American historians are notably reticent about what has happened to democracy in America. They obviously have a great deal to say. But they appear to have given so very little thought to the various meanings that the idea of democracy might have. Perhaps it ought not to have surprised me that American historians, like other Americans, have so little aptitude for, or interest in, what is essentially a problem of political philosophy. But I confess that it did.

Let me give a couple of examples of what I have in mind. If one were to ask, "What is the most effectively conservative piece of legislation passed by the federal government in this century?" the answer, I submit, is both obvious and incontestable. It is the Nineteenth Amendment, extending the suffrage to women. The voting habits of the American population are something we know a great deal about, and there is just no question but that women, to the extent that they do more than duplicate their husbands' votes, are to be found disproportionately in the conservative wing of the electorate. Yet in all our history books the Nineteenth Amendment is regarded as a progressive and liberal action, not at all as a conservative one. This strikes me as being a curious state of affairs and suggests that there is something odd about the way in which Americans go about writing their history.

Another example. If one were to ask, "What is the most effectively conservative piece of legislation passed by state legislatures in this century?" the answer—which I again submit is both obvious and incontestable—is the popular referendum. There must be hundreds of American historians alive today who, in their respective localities, have seen some of their most cherished and most liberal ideas—school integration, for instance, or less restrictive zoning laws—buried in a referendum. Yet when they enter their classrooms, or write their book, all this is forgotten or ignored. Almost invariably they regard the advent of the popular referendum as a victory for both democracy and liberalism. They are very upset when you point out that this seems not to be the case. And they get utterly bewildered if you dare to suggest that based on certain other conceptions of democracy or liberty one need not regard it as a victory for either.

It is clear that something is at work here that is not to be explained by the ordinary canons of historical scholarship. What is involved, it seems to me, is an ideology so powerful as to represent a kind of religious faith. Indeed, we can fairly call this ideology "the democratic faith," since this term is frequently and approvingly used by members of the congregation themselves. Because it is an authentic faith, it is a very complicated and conglomerate affair. But I believe one can say two truthful and simple things about it.

First of all, it evidently cares much more about ascertaining the source and origin of political power than it does about analyzing the existential consequences of this power. Which is to say, like all faiths it places much more emphasis on men's "good" intentions—in this case, men's democratic intentions—than on whatever may follow from these intentions. And, of course, like all faiths it ends up grappling with the problem of evil—with the existence of disorder, and decay, and injustice, which ought not to exist in a society constructed on democratic principles, but which patently do. This problem itself is usually resolved in the traditional religious way—that is, by assuming that it flows from the conspiracy of wicked demiurges ("vested interests," in American jargon) or the undue influence of "alien" ideas that frustrate the perfection we are entitled to.

Second, and this is but a corollary of my first point, what we are dealing with is obviously *not* a political philosophy. The only reason I go to the trouble of pointing this out is that once upon a time, in this country, the question of democracy *was* a matter for political philosophy, rather than for faith. And the way in which a democratic political philosophy was gradually and inexorably transformed into a democratic faith seems to me to be perhaps the most important problem in American intellectual—and ultimately political—history. In this transformation, American historians have played a significant role—although, being themselves for the most part men of good democratic faith, they have been so busy playing this role that they have rarely got around to explaining it to us, or to themselves.

II

The difference between a democratic faith and a democratic political philosophy is basically this: whereas a faith may be attentive to the *problems* of democracy, it has great difficulty perceiving or thinking about the *problematics* of democracy. By "problematics" I mean those kinds of problems that flow from, that are inherent in, that are generated by democracy itself. These problematics change their hue with time and circumstance: the founding fathers would have been as bewildered by the current status of the popular referendum as are our progressive historians. But what makes them problematics rather than problems is that they are organically connected with the political system of democracy itself rather than with any external or adventitious factors.

It really is quite extraordinary how the majority of American historians have, until quite recently, determinedly refused to pay attention to any thinker, or any book, that treated democracy as problematic. Although our historians frequently quote from this source, and much effort has been made to determine who wrote which paper, it is a fact that no American historian has ever written a book on the Federalist Papers. (As a further matter of fact, *no one* in America—historian, political scientist, jurist, or whatever—ever published a book on *The Federalist* until a few years ago, when a Swiss immigrant scholar rather clumsily broke the ice.) Men like E. L. Godkin, Herbert Croly, Paul Elmer More, even Tocqueville, have interested American historians mainly as "source material"— hardly anyone goes to them to *learn* anything about American democracy. And it is certainly no accident that our very greatest historian, Henry Adams, who did indeed understand the problematics of democracy, is a "loner," with no historical school or even a noteworthy disciple to carry on in his tradition. As Richard Hofstadter recently pointed out, there are plenty of Turnerites and Beardites and, of course, Marxists among American historians, but there are no Adamsites or Tocquevillians.

In this respect, the contrast between American historians and the men who created this democracy is a striking one. Although none of the founding fathers can be called a political philosopher, most of them were widely read in political philosophy and had given serious thought to the traditional problems of political philosophy. One of these traditional problems was the problematic character of democracies. The founding fathers were aware that, in centuries past, democracy—in the sense of the unfettered rule of the *demos*, of the majority—had been one of the least stable and not always the most admirable of political regimes. And this awareness—shared by practically all educated men of the time—caused them to devise a system that was more democratic than the "mixed regimes" that most political philosophers approved of, yet that also possessed at least some of the virtues thought to be associated with a "mixed regime." Such virtues pertained not to the *origins* of government but to its *ends*. In short, the founding fathers sought to establish a "popular government" that could be stable, just, free; where there was security of person and property; and whose public leaders would claim legitimacy not only because they were elected officials but also because their character and behavior approximated some accepted models of excellence. The fact that they used the term "popular government" rather than "democracy" is an accident of historical semantics. They were partisans of self-government—of government by the people—who deliberately and with a bold, creative genius "rigged" the machinery of the system so that this government would be one of which they, as thoughtful and civilized men, could be proud.

In establishing such a popular government, the founding fathers were certainly under the impression that they were expressing a faith in the common man. But they were sober and worldly men, and they were not about to hand out blank checks to anyone, even if he was common man. They thought that political institutions had something to do with the shaping of common men, and they took the question, *"What kind of common man does our popular government produce?"* to be as crucial a consideration as any other. They took it for granted that democracy was capable of bringing evil into the world, and they wanted a system of government that made this as unlikely as possible, and that was provided with as strong an inclination toward self-correction as was possible. And I should guess that they would have regarded as a fair test of their labors the degree to which common men in America could rise to the prospect of choosing uncommon men, speaking for uncommon ideals, as worthy of exercising authority over them.

The founding fathers, then, established what they thought to be—and what the world then unanimously thought to be—a democratic process for the American people. But they looked beyond this democratic process to the spirit—the ideal intent—that might animate it. This conception is very nicely expressed in words that Matthew Arnold a century later directed toward his American audiences:

> The difficulty for democracy is, how to find and keep high ideals. The individuals who compose it are, the bulk of them, persons who need to follow an ideal, not to set one; and one ideal of goodness, high feeling, and fine culture, which an aristocracy once supplied to them, they lose by the very fact of ceasing to be a lower order and becoming a democracy. Nations are not truly great solely because the individuals composing them are numerous, free, and active; but they are great when these numbers, this freedom, and this activity are employed in the service of an ideal higher than that of an ordinary man, taken by himself.

These words doubtless sound anachronistic to the ears of those who have in their lifetime heard a President of the United States declare that he would disarm the ideological opponents of democracy by distributing the Sears, Roebuck catalogue among them. But such words would not have sounded strange to the founding fathers, many of whom had occasion to say much the same thing. Between the political philosophy of the founding fathers and the ideology of the

Sears, Roebuck catalogue, there stretches the fascinating—
and still largely untold—story of what happened to the democratic idea in America.

III

In the writing of our first major historian, George Bancroft,
one can already see a clear premonition of things to come.
His was a muted and rather covert operation: the Jacksonians,
of whom Bancroft was one, were not eager to emphasize any
ideological or philosophical differences they might have had
with the founding fathers, whose memory was still revered
among the electorate. Nevertheless, what was involved in Bancroft's work was a giant step toward the redefinition of the
democratic idea. It is striking that in his voluminous writings
Bancroft paid hardly any attention—gave only passing notice
—to the *Federalist*. Indeed, in his *History of the Formation
of the Constitution* he pretty much denied that the founding
fathers had any serious political ideas in their heads at all.
"The men who framed it [the Constitution] followed the
lead of no theoretical writer of their own or preceding
times. . . . They wrought from the elements which were at
hand, and shaped them to meet the new experiences which had
arisen." It was important for Bancroft to assert this, because
he did not want to seem to be taking issue with the founding
fathers in articulating his belief that "the common judgment
in taste, politics, and religion is the highest authority on earth,
and the nearest possible approach to an infallible decision."
Bancroft's strategy was to defend Jacksonian democracy as a
restoration of the original republic in the face of an "aristocratic" conspiracy. It was only if, as Bancroft claimed, the
founding fathers had no political ideas that his own political
ideas could be represented as the natural extension of their

work. In fact, and of course, Bancroft's notion of popular in-fallibility was utterly alien to the founding fathers, and had been explicitly rejected by them.

It was, then, within less than half a century of the founding of the republic that this major revolution in American thought took place, that an original political *philosophy* of democracy was replaced with a religious *faith* in democracy. The sources of this revolution—in theology, in literature, and in politics itself—are not at all mysterious, although they have usually been studied in quite other connections. And the impact of this revolution on American politics and American thought is no mystery, either. Still, the men who were involved in it were usually careful to play down its revolutionary character, and preferred to say—some in all sincerity, others with a seem-ing sincerity that I find suspect—that all they were doing was to draw some natural inferences from the heritage bequeathed to them by the founding fathers.

The nature of this new democratic faith was perhaps most candidly expressed, in political terms, by George Sidney Camp in his book *Democracy* (1841). Camp claimed that his book was the first defense of democracy as the best form of govern-ment for all people, in all places, at all times, ever to be written in the United States. So far as I know, he is absolutely justi-fied in this claim. No man who ever studied political philoso-phy, and seriously contemplated the problems of governing men, had ever said such a thing; certainly none among the founding fathers ever did. But Camp could and did say it be-cause he and his contemporaries had abolished political philos-ophy, to all intents and purposes, and replaced it with a transcendental faith in the common man. The quality of this transcendental faith can be exemplified by quotations from dozens of writers of the time, of which the following—from the senior Henry James, in 1852—is not untypical:

Democracy is not so much a new form of political life as a dissolution and disorganization of old forms. It is simply a resolution of government into the hands of the people, a taking down of that which has before existed, and a recommitment of it to its original sources.

In this mass endeavor at redefining the democratic idea, historians after Bancroft were much less involved than poets, publicists, and men of letters. On the contrary: American historians of the nineteenth century were distinctly more Whiggish and neo-Federalist in their ideological complexion than other classes of writers. Most of them were born in Whiggish households, were engaged in such Whiggish occupations as university education and the law, and had connections with the genteel Brahmin culture of New England and New York. One can understand, therefore, why they were not easy converts to the new transcendental faith of democracy. What is less easy to understand is how most of them—always excepting Adams—managed to dodge any kind of direct confrontation with the transformation of American democracy that was occurring before their very eyes. Perhaps they were intimidated by popular opinion; perhaps, as patriotic Americans, they were reluctant to look too hard and too closely at this matter; perhaps they really did believe that, although the democratic faith clearly represented a departure from the political philosophy of the founding fathers, nevertheless this was a temporary phenomenon, and that ultimately there would be an amiable convergence. Whatever the explanation, however, it is the case that the bulk of nineteenth-century American historiography has about it a curious evasiveness, what one may even call a lack of relevance. (In the case of someone like Parkman, who was perhaps the most gifted of his generation, it is not too harsh to use the term "escapism.") That this is more than a personal impression on my part is indicated by the fact that

American historians of today have little occasion to refer back to these predecessors—and, indeed, most of their writings are out of print.

Such was the situation until the advent of Turner and Beard —at which point, of course, everything changed. Now, for the first time, the historical profession—the official guardians of our civic traditions—made explicit to the American mind what had conveniently been hitherto implicit in American life: the repudiation of the political philosophy of the founding fathers. The shock of recognition that this effected upon the American public was profound and unwelcome.

In browsing through the literature generated by "the Turner thesis" and "the Beard thesis," I am impressed by the way in which most twentieth-century historians have managed to convert an important ideological debate into a matter of academic opinion. Much of this literature centers around the question of whether Turner and Beard were right or wrong in the inferences they drew from their evidence. Only rarely will a historian poke around the premises on which Turner and Beard established their historical writings. Yet it is these premises that are the most interesting and important aspects of their work.

In Turner's writings, the various things he has to say about the frontier are of no great significance compared with the way he uses the term "democracy." After all, no one has ever doubted that the frontier experience had an impact on the American character, that this impact was in the direction of egalitarianism, and that this egalitarianism in turn has had repercussions in all areas of American life. The exact degree of the egalitarian tilt that the frontier, as compared with other influences, did exercise is an issue that may be—and has been—debated. But Turner would hardly have created such a fuss, he would hardly be the major historian he is, if all he had done was to call attention in a somewhat exaggerated fashion to the influence of the frontier. To appreciate Turner's importance, I would argue, one has to see him not so much as a historian as an ideologue; and to understand his work fully, one should regard it as being primarily an ideological enterprise.

The point of this enterprise is indeed to be found in Turner's famous dictum that American democracy was born on the frontier—but that point is not to be found where we have customarily looked at it. Turner was not saying anything terribly novel about the frontier, but he *was* saying something new and important about the way we should use the term "democracy." In effect, he was redefining the democratic idea for the historical profession along lines that had already become familiar outside this profession. He was saying that by "democracy" we ought to mean the Jacksonian-egalitarian-populist transcendental faith in the common man, and he was further explicitly stating that this was something different from, and antithetical to, the kind of democratic political philosophy that the founding fathers believed in. Turner made Americans aware that the conventional republican pieties, which used the word "democracy" as little more than a synonym for "American," were, to say the least, ambiguous. And he offered to young historians the exciting prospect of re-writing American history in the light of a democratic faith.

To get a clear notion of what Turner really did, it is useful to turn to an earlier essay on the relation of the frontier to American democracy. I refer to the essay by E. L. Godkin entitled "Aristocratic Opinions of Democracy," which was published in 1865. The fact that this essay is not much read, and only infrequently referred to, even by historians of American democracy, indicates with what success Turner achieved his true intention—which was, precisely, to make essays like Godkin's as unread and unremembered as possible, even by historians of American democracy.

Godkin's essay is a thoughtful rejoinder to what he took to

be Tocqueville's excessively pessimistic views of the prospects for American democracy. Whether or not Godkin was correct in his interpretation of Tocqueville is here beside the point. In any case, Godkin—who regarded himself as a perfectly good American democrat—was dismayed by what he took to be Tocqueville's assertion that the many virtues of American democracy were incompatible with a high degree of civilization, an elevated culture, and a noble conception of public life. He conceded that these were not yet to be found in America, but attributed their absence to the special material circumstances of American history—*and especially to the continual, pervasive influence of the frontier.* Although Godkin had many kind words for the frontier, he did allow that it was the aggressive, self-seeking individualism, the public disorderliness, the philistine materialism of the American frontier that prevented American democracy from achieving a more splendid destiny. And he held out the hope that, as the influence of the frontier inevitably declined, the quality of American civilization and of American public life would markedly improve.

Now, it is clear that Godkin's idea of democracy was not Turner's—was, indeed, very much at odds with Turner's. It was what we would today designate as a neo-Federalist idea, which regarded egalitarianism as not only an attribute of democracy but also a problem for it, which was very much concerned with seeing to it that the American democracy was deferential to certain high republican ideals—and, of course, to those republican institutions and those "best men" that represented these ideals. Turner never refuted Godkin; Turner—even in his later years, when his feelings about the frontier were mixed—never really tried to come to terms with Godkin; he never really argued, in a serious way, with anyone whose conception of democracy differed from his own. He simply did what all successful ideologues do when they establish a new orthodoxy; he ignored, and persuaded everyone else to ignore, the very existence of these different views—and where this was impossible, he blandly excluded these views from the spectrum of democratic opinion, relocating them on another spectrum vaguely called "aristocratic."

IV

I shall not discuss Charles A. Beard in any detail, since his originality, like Turner's, lay in persuading the historical profession to accept the new ideological redefinition of the democratic idea. Aside from imputing crudely self-interested motives to the founders—a bit of malice that wasn't really crucial to his argument—Beard, so far as I can see, ended up with the aggressive assertion that the founding fathers were not Jacksonian democrats and were men of only partial democratic faith. He was right, of course. The really interesting question is *why* they were not, and whether perhaps they might have had good reason for being what they were. It was not until the end of his life that Beard addressed himself to this question, and in the course of answering it he tacitly abandoned his original thesis. But, by this time, American historians had naturally ceased being interested in Beard.

Nor shall I say anything more about the "progressive" school of historical scholarship that has been the dominant orthodoxy of these past six decades. I am sure I have made it sufficiently clear that, whatever the merits—and they are often considerable—of particular "progressive" historians, their work seems to me crucially deficient by virtue of their *simpliste* conception of democracy. I find too much theodicy in their writings, and too little political philosophy. I have learned much from them—but only rarely have I learned what they set out to teach me.

As one might expect, I am far more sympathetic to the work of the so-called "revisionists"—such men as Richard Hofstadter, Marvin Meyers, Stanley Elkins, and others—who have perceived that the democratic faith of progressive historiography does not really square with the facts of our democratic history. These are the historians of my lifetime whom I find most instructive and most "relevant." And yet in the end I have to conclude that even they are curiously unsatisfying. They trouble me because they are, precisely, "revisionists" in their attitude and perspective. That is to say, they are excellent in pointing out the shortcomings of the standard, "progressive" account of such historical phenomena as Jacksonianism, abolitionism, populism. But it is never clear to me what they would put in its place—or whether, indeed, they really want to go so far as to put anything new in its place. They seem to see their task as primarily corrective, and while their corrections strike me as persuasive and pertinent, such revisionism leaves me with the feeling that many important things—perhaps even the most important things—remain to be said.

It is true that a few scholars, sometimes counted very loosely among the "revisionists," *have* offered such a perspective and general statement. But this only reinforces my uneasiness. Thus, in reacting against the notion that American history can be seen as one long conflict between those of true democratic faith and an ever-incipient "aristocratic" reaction, Daniel Boorstin has emphasized—quite correctly, in my view—the "consensus" in political attitudes that most Americans have, throughout their history, subscribed to. For him, the relative immunity of our society to ideological speculation is a fortunate circumstance, and he quotes with approval Edmund Burke:

The bulk of mankind on their part are not excessively curious concerning any theories, whilst they are really happy; and one sure symptom of an ill-conducted state is the propensity of the people to resort to them.

Now I happen to agree with both Burke and Boorstin on the truth of this proposition. I dislike ideologically turbulent societies because they have a tendency to barbarize men who may previously have been at least modestly civilized, and to primitivize ideas that may previously have been at least modestly fine and complex. But I would go on to note that Boorstin is reading Burke carelessly, and that Burke does not mean what Boorstin seems to think he does. Burke, in this quotation, is talking about "the bulk of mankind" and "the people." He was *not* talking about political philosophers or historians or scholars—he was, after all, one himself. Burke thought it was a disaster when political philosophies became popular ideologies. But he never meant to suggest that truly thoughtful men should not engage in political philosophy, and one can hardly doubt that he valued political philosophy and political philosophers very highly. Burke could not have had a high regard for a society where *no one* was engaging in the serious study of politics—a study that was, for him, one of the noblest of human enterprises. In short, I do not think Burke, were he alive today, would regard the history of American democracy with quite the same satisfaction that Boorstin does. He might even be somewhat appalled at the enduring *mindlessness* of this democracy.

Professor Louis Hartz has also a new and general interpretation of American history. But there is an interesting difference between Hartz and Boorstin. Where Boorstin emphasizes the *non*-ideological character of American democracy, Hartz emphasizes its *uni*-ideological character. He, too, stresses the extent to which American political opinion has represented an enduring consensus, but this time it is around an idea, and does not merely reflect, as in Boorstin, a "pragmatic" adaptation to life on the American continent. The idea—the American liberal-democratic idea—is compounded of a few Lockean dogmas. And the history of American thought is little more than the changes rung—the permutations and combinations—within this idea.

Anyone who is even reasonably familiar with European history over these past two centuries cannot doubt the validity of this thesis—cannot doubt that, in comparison with Europe, America has had a remarkable homogeneity of ideology. But what is truly astonishing is that Hartz, after demonstrating the dominion of Lockean ideology, proceeds to insist that ideology itself is of no importance anyway. "The system of democracy," he tells us, "works by virtue of certain processes which its theory never describes, to which, indeed, its theory is actually hostile." This process involves "group coercion, crowd psychology, and economic power"; out of the push and pull of conflicting interests, there emerges an equilibrium that represents a kind of gross public interest. If and when we examine the ideology of this democratic process, and find it faulty or deficient, this is a crisis of democracy's image, not of its reality—a mere "agony of the mind rather than of the real world."

I must say that I was taken aback when Hartz, who is an intellectual historian of considerable talent and insight, led me to this conclusion. Only in America, I thought, could a historian of ideas—whose major work reveals the very great influence that a particular version of the democratic idea has had upon our history—end up with the assertion that political mind has no dominion over political matter. That the statement is false on the basis of Hartz's own work bothers me less than the fact that it is false in general—I honestly don't see how any intelligent man with even the slightest bit of worldly experience could entertain this belief. The political ideas that men have *always* help to shape the political reality they live in—and this is so whether these be habitual opinions, tacit convictions, or explicit ideologies. It is ideas that establish and define in men's minds the categories of the politically possible and the politically impossible, the desirable and the undesirable, the tolerable and the intolerable. And what is more ultimately real, politically, than the structure of man's political imagination? Hartz's own book reveals that there is nothing more real; and his book will survive the rather bewildering lessons he has managed to learn from it.

Reading Boorstin and Hartz, one comes away with the strong impression that America has been a very lucky country. I do not doubt this for a moment. But unless one is willing to claim that this luck is a sign of an enduring Divine benevolence —unless one believes that Americans are indeed sons of the Covenant, a chosen people—it is very difficult to argue from the fact of luck to the notion that democracy in America is a *good* form of government, or that we have more than an expediential commitment to this form of government. And while, as I have said, I recognize America's good luck, I really cannot believe that Americans are a historically unique and chosen people. I am myself a Jew and an American, and with all due respect to the Deity, I think the odds are prohibitive that He would have gone out of His way to choose me twice over.

V

Lucky we have been, but perhaps our luck is beginning to run out. I believe that all of us are well aware that the areas of American life that are becoming unstable and problematic are increasing in numbers and size every day. Yet our initial response—and it usually remains our final response—is to echo

Al Smith: "All the ills of democracy can be cured by more democracy." But is this really true? Is it true of our mass media, of our political party system, of our foreign policy, of our crisis in race relations? Is it not possible that many of the ills of our democracy can be traced to this democracy itself—or, more exactly, to this democracy's conception of itself? And how are we even to contemplate this possibility if our historians seem so unaware of it?

It appears to me that there is a great deal of work still to be done in American history. To begin with, one would like to know *why* the political philosophy of the founding fathers was so ruthlessly unmanned by American history. Was it the result of inherent flaws in that political philosophy itself? Was it a failure of statesmanship? Was it a consequence of external developments that were unpredictable and uncontrollable? These questions have hardly been asked, let alone answered. And the reason they haven't been asked is, first of all, the dominance of the progressive historian, who sees American history in terms of an ineluctable and providential "Rise of the Common Man," and, second, that even the revisionists shy away from raising the basic issues of political philosophy that are involved.

I should like to think that I am as good a democrat as the average historian, with as genuine an affection for the common man. But unlike the "consensus historians," I do not see that the condition of American democracy is such as automatically to call forth my love and honor, although I respect it enough to offer it my obedience. And unlike the so-called "conflict historians," I get no relief in discovering as many instances as possible of civil strife and mob disorder. Both of these schools of thought, it seems to me, perceive the common man—the one in his potential for merely self-centered activity, the other in his exclusive potential for resisting authority—in terms that remind me of Ortega's definition of the "mass man": the individual who is not capable of assuming responsibility for self-limitation, for a kind of self-definition that is both generous and self-respecting. Interestingly enough, Ortega's definition of the "mass man" is identical with Plato's definition of the tyrant. Which in turn suggests that the idea of the tyranny of the majority—whether it be an essentially mindless, self-seeking majority or a simply rancorous one—is capable of more general application than has hitherto been thought to be the case. And this, in its turn, leads me to wonder whether American historians themselves have not too frequently, and all too willingly, fallen victim to what is ultimately a tyrannical vulgarization of the democratic idea.

5

American Intellectuals and Foreign Policy

A RECENT LETTER to the *New York Times*, complaining about the role of the academic community in opposing the government's Vietnam policy, argued that "it is not clear why people trained in mathematics, religion, geology, music, etc., believe their opinions on military and international problems should carry much validity." And the letter went on: "Certainly they [the professors] would oppose unqualified Pentagon generals telling them how to teach their course."

One can understand this complaint; one may even sympathize with the sentiments behind it. The fact remains, however, that it does miss the point. For the issue is not intellectual competence or intellectual validity—not really, and despite all protestations to the contrary. What is at stake is that species of power we call moral authority. The intellectual critics of American foreign policy obviously and sincerely believe that their arguments are right. But it is clear they believe, even more obviously and sincerely, that *they* are right—and that the totality of this rightness amounts to much more than the sum of the individual arguments.

An intellectual may be defined as a man who speaks with general authority about a subject on which he has no particular competence. This definition sounds ironic, but is not. The authority is real enough, just as the lack of specific competence is crucial. An economist writing about economics is not acting as an intellectual, nor is a literary critic when he explicates a text. In such cases, we are witnessing professionals at work. On the other hand, there is good reason why we ordinarily take the "man of letters" as the archetypical intellectual. It is he who most closely resembles his sociological forebear and ideal type: the sermonizing cleric.

Precisely which people, at which time, in any particular social situation, are certified as "intellectuals" is less important than the fact that such certification is achieved—informally but indisputably. And this process involves the recognition of the intellectual as legitimately possessing the prerogative of being moral guide and critic to the world. (It is not too much of an exaggeration to say that even the clergy in the modern world can claim this prerogative only to the extent that it apes the intellectual class. It is the "writing cleric," like the "writing psychoanalyst," who achieves recognition.) But there is this critical difference between the intellectual of today and the average cleric of yesteryear: the intellectual, lacking in other-worldly interests, is committed to the pursuit of temporal status, temporal influence, and temporal power with a single-minded passion that used to be found only in the highest reaches of the Catholic Church. Way back in 1797, Benjamin Constant observed that "in the new society where the prestige of rank is destroyed, we—thinkers, writers, and philosophers—should be honored as the first among all citizens." The only reason Constant did not say "we intellectuals" is that the term had not yet come into common usage.

It is simply not possible to comprehend what is happening in the United States today unless one keeps the sociological condition and political ambitions of the intellectual class very much in the forefront of one's mind. What we have been witnessing is no mere difference of opinion about foreign policy, or about Vietnam. Such differences of opinion do exist, of course. Some of the most articulate critics believe that the United States has, through bureaucratic inertia and mental sloth, persisted in a foreign policy that, whatever its relevance to the immediate postwar years, is by now dangerously anachronistic. They insist that the United States has unthinkingly accepted world responsibilities which are beyond its resources and that, in any case, these responsibilities have only an illusory connection with the enduring national interest. These men may be right, or they may be wrong. But right or wrong, *this* debate is largely irrelevant to the convulsion that the American intellectual community is now going through—even though occasional references may be made to it, for credibility's sake. One does not accuse the President of the United States and the Secretary of State of being "war criminals" and "mass murderers" because they have erred in estimating the proper dimensions of the United States' overseas commitments. And it is precisely accusations of this kind that are inflaming passions on the campus, and which are more and more coming to characterize the "peace movement" as a whole.

What we are observing is a phenomenon that is far more complex in its origins and far-reaching in its implications. It involves, among other things, the highly problematic relationship of the modern intellectual to foreign affairs, the basic self-definition of the American intellectual, the tortured connections between American liberal ideology and the American imperial republic, and the role of the newly established academic classes in an affluent society. Above all, it raises the question of whether democratic societies can cope with the kinds of political pathologies that seem to be spontaneously generated by their very commitment to economic and social progress.

II

No modern nation has ever constructed a foreign policy that was acceptable to its intellectuals. True, at moments of national peril or national exaltation, intellectuals will feel the same patriotic emotions as everyone else, and will subscribe as enthusiastically to the common cause. But these moments pass, the process of disengagement begins, and it usually does not take long for disengagement to eventuate in alienation. Public opinion polls generally reveal that the overwhelming majority of ordinary citizens, at any particular time, will be approving of their government's foreign policy; among intellectuals, this majority tends to be skimpy at best, and will frequently not exist at all. It is reasonable to suppose that there is an instinctive bias at work here, favorable to government among the common people, unfavorable among the intellectuals.

The bias of the common man is easy to understand: he is never much interested in foreign affairs; his patriotic feelings incline him to favor his own government against the governments of foreigners; and in cases of international conflict, he is ready to sacrifice his self-interest for what the government assures him to be the common good. The persistent bias of intellectuals, on the other hand, requires some explaining.

We have noted that the intellectual lays claim—and the claim is, more often than not, recognized—to moral authority over the intentions and actions of political leaders. This claim finds concrete rhetorical expression in an ideology. What creates a community of intellectuals, as against a mere aggregate of individuals, is the fact that they subscribe—with varying degrees of warmth, or with more or less explicit reservations—to a prevailing ideology. This ideology permits them to interpret the past, make sense of the present, outline a shape for the future. It constitutes the essence of their rationality, as this is directed toward the life of man in society.

Now, it is the peculiarity of foreign policy that it is the area of public life in which ideology flounders most dramatically. Thus, while it is possible—if not necessarily fruitful—to organize the political writings of the past three hundred years along a spectrum ranging from the ideological left to the ideological right, no such arrangement is conceivable for writings on foreign policy. There is no great radical text on the conduct of foreign policy—and no great conservative text, either. What texts there are (e.g., Machiavelli, Grotius, in our own day the writings of George Kennan and Hans Morgenthau) are used indifferently by all parties, as circumstance allows.

And we find, if we pursue the matter further, that the entire tradition of Western political thought has very little to say about foreign policy. From Thucydides to our own time, political philosophy has seen foreign affairs as so radically affected by contingency, fortune, and fate as to leave little room for speculative enlightenment. John Locke was fertile in suggestions for the establishment and maintenance of good government, but when it came to foreign affairs he pretty much threw up his hands:

What is to be done in reference to foreigners, depending much upon their actions and the variation of designs and interests, must be left in great part to the prudence of those who have this power committed to them, to be managed by the best of their skill for the advantage of the Commonwealth.

The reasons why this should be so are not mysterious. To begin with, the very idea of "foreign policy" is so amorphous as to be misleading. As James Q. Wilson has pointed out, it is not at all clear that a state department can have a foreign policy in a meaningful sense of that term—i.e., one "policy" that encompasses our economic, military, political, and sentimental relations with nations neighborly or distant, friendly or inimical. Moreover, whereas a national community is governed by principles by which one takes one's intellectual and moral bearings, the nations of the world do not constitute such a community and propose few principles by which their conduct may be evaluated. What this adds up to is that ideology can obtain exasperatingly little purchase over the realities of foreign policy—and that intellectuals feel keenly their dispossession from this area. It is not that intellectuals actually believe—though they often assert it—that the heavy reliance upon expediency in foreign affairs is intrinsically immoral. It is just that this reliance renders intellectuals as a class so much the less indispensable: to the extent that expediency is a necessary principle of action, to that extent the sovereignty of intellectuals is automatically circumscribed. It is only where politics is ideologized that intellectuals have a pivotal social and political role. To be good at coping with expediential situations you don't have to be an intellectual—and it may even be a handicap.

It is this state of affairs that explains the extraordinary inconsistencies of intellectuals on matters of foreign policy, and the ease with which they can enunciate a positive principle, only in the next breath to urge a contrary action. So it is that many intellectuals are appalled at our military intervention in Southeast Asia, on the grounds that no matter what happens there the national security of the United States will not be threatened. But these same intellectuals would raise no objection if the United States sent an expeditionary force all the way to South Africa to overthrow apartheid, even though South Africa offers no threat to American security. So it is, too, that intellectual critics are fond of accusing American foreign policy of neglecting "political solutions" in favor of crude military and economic action—thereby demonstrating their faith that if foreign policy were suffused with sufficient ideological rationality it would dissolve the recalcitrance that mere statesmen encounter. And when the statesman candidly responds that he is coping not with problems but with an endless series of crises, and that he really has no way of knowing beforehand what "solution," if any, is feasible, he is simply reinforcing the intellectual's conviction that the managers of foreign affairs are, if not more wicked than he is, then certainly more stupid. Usually, he will be willing to think they are both.

Charles Frankel has written that "international affairs are peculiarly susceptible to galloping abstractions"* and has stressed that "intellectuals, more than most other groups, have the power to create, dignify, inflate, criticize, moderate or puncture these abstractions." In the event, intellectuals rarely moderate or puncture, but are diligent in inflation. Abstractions are their life's blood, and even when they resolutely decide to become "tough-minded" they end up with an oversimplified ideology of Realpolitik that is quite useless as a guide to the conduct of foreign affairs and leads its expounders to one self-contradiction after another. But the important point is not that intellectuals are always wrong on matters of foreign policy—they are not, and could not possibly be, if only by the laws of chance. What is striking is that, right or wrong, they are so often, from the statesman's point of view, irrelevant. And it is their self-definition as ideological creatures that makes them so.

III

In the United States, this ideological self-definition has taken on a very special form, and the relation of the American intellectual to foreign policy has its own distinctive qualities. Just

* Charles Frankel, "The Scribblers and International Relations," *Foreign Affairs,* October 1965.

how distinctive may be gathered from asking oneself the following question: Is it conceivable that American intellectuals should *ever* disapprove of *any* popular revolution, anywhere in the world—whatever the express or implicit principles of this revolution? One can make this question even sharper: Is it conceivable for American intellectuals ever to approve of their government suppressing, or helping to frustrate, any popular revolution *by poor people*—whatever the nature or consequences of this revolution? The answer would obviously have to be in the negative; and the implications of this answer for American foreign policy are not insignificant. This policy must work within a climate of opinion that finds the idea of a *gradual* evolution of traditional societies thoroughly uninteresting—which, indeed, has an instinctive detestation of all traditional societies as being inherently unjust, and an equally instinctive approval, as being inherently righteous, of any revolutionary ideology which claims to incorporate the people's will.

As a matter of fact, even though official policy must obviously be based on other considerations, the makers of policy themselves find it nearly impossible to escape from this ideological framework. The State Department, for example, is always insisting that the United States is a truly revolutionary society, founded on revolutionary principles and offering a true revolutionary promise—as contrasted with the communists' spurious promises. The intellectual critics of American foreign policy deny that any such revolutionary intention or program exists—but think it ought to. There are precious few people in the United States who will say aloud that revolutionary intentions are inconsistent with a prudent and responsible foreign policy of a great power. Oddly enough, to hear this point made with some urgency these days, one has to go to the Soviet Union.

The American intellectual tradition has two profound commitments: to "ideals" and to "the people." It is the marriage of these two themes that has made the American mind and given it its characteristic cast—which might be called *transcendentalist populism.*

The "transcendentalist" theme in American thought is linked to a disrespect for tradition, a suspicion of all institutionalized authority, an unshakable faith in the "natural" (what once was called "divine") wisdom of the sincere individual, an incorruptible allegiance to one's own "inner light." The American intellectual sees himself as being in perpetual "prophetic confrontation" with principalities and powers. (That very phrase, "prophetic confrontation," has lately been used by Hans Morgenthau to define the proper stance of the intellectual vis-à-vis his government's policies.) Tell an American intellectual that he is a disturber of the intellectual peace, and he is gratified. Tell him he is a reassuring spokesman for calm and tranquillity, and he will think you have made a nasty accusation.

This transcendentalist "protestantism" of the American intellectual derives from the history of American Protestantism itself—as does his near-mystical celebration of "the people." Indeed, the two themes have evolved as part of one historical process, which has been concisely described by the historian Russell B. Nye:

From the mid-18th century to the mid-19th in American thought . . . the accepted version of the individual's power to grasp and interpret God's truth underwent a complete change— from Calvin's dependence on the Bible . . . to Deism's grant to man of equal sovereignty in a universe of reason, to Channing's transfer of sovereignty from Bible and church to man, and finally to the *self*-reliance of Emerson, Parker, and Thoreau. The lines of thought moved from Mather's distrust of man, to Jefferson's qualified confidence in him, to Emerson's and Jackson's deep and abiding faith in his capacity to find out and act upon divine truth.*

This evolution, which might be called the democratization of the spirit, has created an American intellectual who is at one and the same time (a) humble toward an idealized and mythical prototype of the common man (if the people have a quasi-ecclesiastical function, to oppose them in any consistent way partakes of heresy) and (b) arrogant toward existing authority, as presumptively representing nothing but a petrified form of yesteryear's vital forces. It has also had a peculiar effect upon the politics of American intellectuals, which is more often than not a kind of transcendentalist politics, focusing less on the reform of the polity than on the perfection and purification of self in opposition to the polity. Just as the intellectual opposition to slavery in the 1830's and 1840's paid little attention to the reform of particular institutions but focused primarily on the need for the individual to avoid being compromised and contaminated by this general evil, so in the 1960's what appeared most to torment our academic intellectuals was the morality of their own actions—whether they should cooperate with Selective Service, accept government contracts, pay taxes, etc. At both times, the issue of individual, conscientious "civil disobedience" became acute. It is instructive to note that, though the British Labor Party bitterly opposed British imperialism for over five decades, its opposition never took any such form. This is some measure of the difference between a political tradition and one that transcends mere politics.

The United States, to be sure, does have its own political tradition. And though the American intellectual tradition has

* Russell B. Nye, "The Search for the Individual, 1750–1850," *The Centennial Review*, Winter 1961.

suffused all areas of American life, it has never completely overwhelmed the political. This latter, mainly the creation of American Whiggery, is incarnated in our major institutions and finds its literary expression in such documents as the Constitution, the Federalist Papers, some Presidential addresses, judicial decisions, etc. This tradition is still very much alive in our law schools and helps explain why these schools play so singular a role in our political life. But among intellectuals it has never enjoyed much favor, being thought to be inherently conservative and nondemocratic. The American intellectual of today is far more comfortable listening to a "protest folk song"—the truly indigenous art form of transcendental populism—than he is listening to a grave and solemn debate over a matter of policy. Witness the way in which the one genre has overwhelmed the other in the "teach-in."

Precisely what an American intellectual does *not* believe was most elegantly expressed by Sir Thomas More, in the discussion of an intellectual's obligation in his *Utopia:*

> If evil persons cannot be quite rooted out, and if you cannot correct habitual attitudes as you wish, you must not therefore abandon the commonwealth. . . . You must strive to guide policy indirectly, so that you make the best of things, and what you cannot turn to good, you can at least make less bad. For it is impossible to do all things well unless all men are good, and this I do not expect to see for a long time.

There have been, of course, some American intellectuals who have followed Sir Thomas More's direction. For their efforts and pains, they have been subjected to the scorn and contempt of the intellectual community as a whole. (Arthur Schlesinger, Jr., Eric Goldman, and John Roche could provide us with eloquent testimony on this score.) This community, unlike Sir Thomas More, is quite convinced that all men are indeed good and that any such modest and compromising

involvement with political power can represent only a corruption of the spirit.

I V

The transformation of the American republic into an imperial
power has sharply exacerbated the relations between the intellectual and the makers of foreign policy. The term "imperial
power" is merely a synonym for "great power" and is not
necessarily the same thing as "imperialistic" power. But there
would seem to be a gain in clarity, and a diminution of hum-
bug, in insisting on the use of the more provocative phrase.
There are a great many people who appear to think that a great
power is only the magnification of a small power, and that
the principles governing the actions of the latter are simply
transferrable—perhaps with some modification—to the former. In fact, there is a qualitative difference between the two
conditions, and the difference can be summed up as follows:
a great power is "imperial" because what it does *not* do is just
as significant, and just as consequential, as what it does. Which
is to say, a great power does not have the range of freedom
of action—derived from the freedom of inaction—that a small
power possesses. It is entangled in a web of responsibilities
from which there is no hope of escape; and its policy-makers
are doomed to a strenuous and unquiet life, with no prospect
of ultimate resolution, no hope for an unproblematic existence,
no promise of final contentment. It is understandable that
these policy-makers should sometimes talk as if some particular
redirection of policy, of any great power, is capable of termi-
nating the tensions inherent in this imperial condition. But it
is foolish for us to believe them; and it is even more foolish for
them to believe themselves. It is no accident that all classical
political philosophers, and all depicters of utopia, have agreed

that to be truly happy a human community should be relatively small and as isolated as possible from foreign entanglements.

Indeed, this utopian ideal is a major historic theme of American foreign policy, being at the root of what we call "isolationism." And as long as the United States was not a great power, it was not entirely utopian. The American republic, until the beginning of the twentieth century, was genuinely isolationist, and isolationism made both practical and idealistic sense. Practical sense because the United States was geographically isolated from the main currents of world politics. Idealistic sense because the United States could feel—and it was no illusion—that it served as a splendid and inspiring example to all believers in popular government everywhere, and that this exemplary role was more important than any foreign actions it might undertake, with the limited resources at its command. True, at the same time that the United States was isolationist, it was also expansionist. But there is no necessary contradiction between these two orientations, even though some modern historians are shocked to contemplate their coexistence. Most of the territories that the United States coveted, and all that were acquired, prior to the Civil War, were thinly populated—there was no subjugation of large, alien masses. And the intent of this expansion was always to incorporate such territories into the United States on absolutely equal terms, not to dominate them for any reasons of state. The idea of "manifest destiny" was therefore easily reconcilable to the isolationist idea. This reconciliation became troublesome only when expansion threatened to disturb the regional balance of power within the republic. Thus, the opposition to the Mexican War among some Northerners was intense, because it meant a possible accretion to the power of the "slavocracy." But there would otherwise have been little opposition to westward and southwestward expansion; and, once the war was over, no one thought for a moment of giving these territories back to Mexico or permitting them to evolve into independent national entities.

In the end, of course, "manifest destiny" did write an end to American isolationism, by establishing the material conditions for the emergence of the United States as a great power. But the isolationist idea, or at least crucial aspects of it, survived—not simply as some kind of "cultural lag" but by reason of being intimately conjoined to "the American way of life" and to the American intellectual creed. This way of life insisted upon the subordination of public policy to private, individual needs and concerns. It had little use for the idea of military glory, which Abraham Lincoln called "that attractive rainbow that rises in showers of blood—that serpent's eye that charms to destroy." It was intensely patriotic, but allergic to all conceptions of national grandeur. The United States was tempted to a brief fling at European-style imperialism under Presidents McKinley and Theodore Roosevelt, but found the experience disagreeable, and that enterprise was gradually liquidated. When the American democracy entered World War I, it was in no imperial frame of mind. On the contrary, the whole point of the Wilsonian "crusade" was to rid the world of imperial politics. One can almost say that this crusade was a penultimate outburst of the isolationist spirit, in that its goal was a happy, self-determined existence for all the individuals on this earth—*une vie à l'Américaine*—without any further cruel violations of it by international power politics.

The disillusionment consequent upon this crusade prepared the way for the United States to enter history as an imperial power. To be sure, its most immediate effect was to stimulate a purely geographic isolationism that was shot through with streaks of xenophobia. But this attitude simply could not withstand the pressure of events and the insistent demands of world realities. In retrospect, the spectacle of the United States entering World War II has an almost dreamlike, fatalistic quality. There was never, prior to Pearl Harbor, any literal threat to the national security of the United States. And there was no popular enthusiasm, except among a small if influential group of "internationalists," for the United States' accepting responsibility for the maintenance of "world order." It all just seemed inescapable, and the alternative—retiring into a Fortress America—just too unmanly. The dominant mood was resignation, tinged with outrage at the Japanese bombardment of American soil. And resignation—sometimes sullen, sometimes equable—has remained the dominant popular mood ever since.

Strangely enough, this resigned acceptance of great-power responsibilities by the American people has been accompanied by a great unease on the part of the intellectuals. It is strange, because one had expected the reverse of this situation. During the two postwar decades, many commentators expressed doubt whether the American people could sustain the frustrations and sacrifices inherent in an imperial role. Such doubts were given point by the upsurge of extremist sentiments associated with the late Senator McCarthy, and unquestionably incited by popular resentment at the Korean War. But Korea can now be seen to have been a kind of baptism-by-fire; and the war in Vietnam has been borne with greater patience than might have been expected. It has not been a popular war—how could it be? —but the general feeling was that it had to be endured. It is among the intellectuals—including some of the aforementioned commentators—that extreme dissatisfaction, sometimes extremist dissatisfaction, is rife. It is among American intellectuals that the isolationist ideal is experiencing its final, convulsive agony.

Though this dissatisfaction affects only a minority, it is

nevertheless a most serious matter. It is much to be doubted that the United States can continue to play an imperial role without the endorsement of its intellectual class. Or, to put it more precisely: since there is no way the United States, as the world's mightiest power, can avoid such an imperial role, the opposition of its intellectuals means that this role will be played out in a domestic climate of ideological dissent that will enfeeble the resolution of our statesmen and diminish the credibility of their policies abroad.

What is to be done? It is always possible to hope that this intellectual class will come to realize that its traditional ideology needs reformation and revision. It is even possible to argue plausibly that, in the nature of things, this is "historically inevitable." One can go so far as to say that, on intellectual grounds alone, this intellectual class will feel moved to desist from the shrill enunciation of pieties and principles that have little relevance to the particular cases our statesmen now confront, and to help formulate a new set of more specific principles that will relate the ideals which sustain the American democracy to the harsh and nasty imperatives of imperial power. All of this is possible. But one must add that none of these possibilities is likely to be realized in the immediate or even near future.

It is unlikely for two reasons. The first is that the burden of guilt such a process would generate would be so great as to be insupportable. It took three centuries to create the American intellectual as we know him today; he is not going to be re-created in one generation. He is committed in the most profound way to a whole set of assumptions and ideas that are rooted in the "isolationist" era of American history, and he cannot depart from these assumptions and ideals without a terrible sense of self-betrayal. Our State Department may find it necessary, if disagreeable, to support military dictatorships in certain countries, at certain times. It is hard to see our intellectuals swallowing this necessity. They might agree in the abstract that alternatives are not available. They might even grant to certain dictatorships the kind of dispensation that is often extended to heathens by an otherwise dogmatic orthodoxy. But they will gag at extending such a dispensation to "our" dictators—this would be too subversive of the dogmas by which they define their existence as a class. The furthest that American intellectuals can go toward coping with the realities of imperial power is to erect a double standard that undermines the moral basis of American diplomacy.

Second, this crisis of the intellectual class in the face of an imperial destiny coincides with an internal power struggle within the United States itself. Our intellectuals are moving toward a significant "confrontation" with the American "establishment" and will do nothing to strengthen the position of their antagonist. Which is to say that the American intellectual class actually has an interest in thwarting the evolution of any kind of responsible and coherent imperial policy. Just what this interest is, and what this confrontation involves, we are only now beginning to discern. Behind the general fog that the ideology of dissent generates, the outlines of a very material sociological and political problem are emerging.

V

It has always been assumed that as the United States became a more highly organized national society, as its economy became more managerial, its power more imperial, and its populace more sophisticated, the intellectuals would move inexorably closer to the seats of authority—would, perhaps, even be incorporated en masse into a kind of "power elite." Many writers and thinkers—and not only on the political left—have viewed this prospect with the greatest unease, for it seemed to them to threaten the continued existence of intellectuals as a critical and moral force in American life.

Well, it has happened here—only, as is so often the case, it is all very different from what one expected. It is true that a small section of the American intellectual class has become a kind of permanent brain trust to the political, the military, the economic authorities. These are the men who commute regularly to Washington, who help draw up programs for reorganizing the bureaucracy, who evaluate proposed weapons systems, who figure out ways to improve our cities and assist our poor, who analyze the course of economic growth, who reckon the cost and effectiveness of foreign aid programs, who dream up new approaches to such old social problems as the mental health of the aged, etc., etc. But what has also happened, at the same time, is that a whole new intellectual class has emerged as a result of the explosive growth, in these past decades, of higher education in the United States. And these "new men," so far from being any kind of elite, are a mass—and have engendered their own mass movement.

As a matter of courtesy and habit, one refers to these professors as "intellectuals." Some of them, of course, are intellectuals, in the traditional sense of the term. The majority unquestionably are not—no population, no matter how elevated, could produce *that many* intellectuals. Professor Robert Nisbet, as shrewd an observer of the academic scene as we have, has estimated that "at the present time not less than sixty percent of all academics in the universities in this country have so profound a distaste for the classroom and for the pains of genuine scholarship or creative thought that they will seize upon anything . . . to exempt themselves respectably from each."*

In most instances, whether a man these days ends up a college

---

* Robert A. Nisbet, "What Is an Intellectual?" *Commentary*, December 1965.

professor or, say, a social worker or a civil servant is largely a matter of chance. Nevertheless, this academic mass has taken over not only the political metaphysics of the American intellectual, but also his status and prerogatives. Americans have always had a superstitious, if touching, faith in the importance of education. And the American people have quickly conceded to the professoriat of our affluent society the moral authority that intellectuals have always claimed as their peculiar endowment.

Now, this new intellectual class, though to outsiders appearing to be not at all badly off, is full of grievance and resentment. It feels discriminated against—opinion polls reveal that professors, especially in the social sciences and humanities, invariably tend drastically to underestimate the esteem in which public opinion (and, more particularly, the opinion of the business community) holds them. It feels underpaid; you'll not find any credence on the campus for the proposition (demonstrably true) that the salaries of professors compare favorably with the salaries of bank executives. It feels put upon in all sorts of other familiar ways. The symptoms are only too typical: here is a new class that is "alienated" from the established order because it feels that this order has not conceded to it sufficient power and recognition.

The politics of this new class is novel in that its locus of struggle is the college campus. One is shocked at this—we are used to thinking that politics ought not to intrude on the campus. But we shall no doubt get accustomed to the idea. Meanwhile, there is going to be a great deal of unpleasant turbulence. The academic community in the United States today has evolved into a new political constituency. College students, like their teachers, are "new men" who find the traditional student role too restrictive. Students and faculty therefore find it easy to combine their numbers and their energies for the purpose of social and political action. The first objective—already accomplished in large measure—is to weaken control of the administration and to dispossess it of its authoritative powers over campus activities. From this point the movement into politics proper—including elections—is about as predictable as anything can be.

Just what direction this movement into politics will follow it is too early to say with certainty. Presumably, it will be toward the left, since this is the historical orientation of the intellectual class as a whole. It is even possible that the movement will not be calmed until the United States has witnessed the transformation of its two-party system to make room for a mass party of the ideological left, as in most European countries—except that its grass roots will be on the campus rather than in the factory. But what is certain is that the national prestige and the international position of the United States are being adversely affected by this *sécession des clercs*. Imperial powers need social equilibrium at home if they are to act effectively in the world. It was possible to think, in the years immediately after World War II, that the United States had indeed achieved this kind of equilibrium—that consensus and equipoise at home would permit our statesmen to formulate and pursue a coherent foreign policy. But the "academic revolution" of the 1950's and 1960's raises this issue again, in a most problematic and urgent way.

VI

Though there is much fancy rhetoric, pro and con, about "the purpose of American foreign policy," there is really nothing esoteric about this purpose. The United States wishes to establish and sustain a world order that (a) ensures its national security as against the other great powers, (b) encourages other nations, especially the smaller ones, to mold their social, political, and economic institutions along lines that are at least not repugnant to (if not actually congruent with) American values, and (c) minimizes the possibility of naked, armed conflict. This is, of course, also the purpose of the foreign policies of such other great powers as Soviet Russia and Maoist China. Nor could it be otherwise, short of a fit of collective insanity on the part of the governing classes of these powers. Without the conflict, tension and reconciliation of such imperial purposes there would be no such thing as "foreign affairs" or "world politics," as we ordinarily understand these terms.

But for any imperial policy to work effectively—even if one means by that nothing more than doing the least possible mischief—it needs intellectual and moral guidance. It needs such guidance precisely because, in foreign affairs, one is always forced to compromise one's values. In the United States today, a relative handful of intellectuals proffers such guidance to the policy-maker. But the intellectual community en masse, disaffected from established power even as it tries to establish a power base of its own, feels no such sense of responsibility. It denounces, it mocks, it vilifies—and even if one were to concede that its fierce indignation was justified by extraordinary ineptitude in high places, the fact remains that its activity is singularly unhelpful. The United States is not going to cease being an imperial power, no matter what happens in Vietnam or elsewhere. It is the world situation—and the history which created this situation—that appoints imperial powers, not anyone's decision or even anyone's overweening ambition. And power begets responsibility—above all, the responsibility to use this power responsibly. The policy-maker in the United States today—and, no doubt, in the other great powers, too—finds this responsibility a terrible burden. The intellectuals, in contrast, are bemused by dreams of power without responsibility, even as they complain of moral responsibility without power. It is not a healthy situation; and, as of this moment, it must be said that one cannot see how, or where, or when it will all end.

6

"When Virtue Loses All Her Loveliness" —Some Reflections on Capitalism and "The Free Society"

W HEN WE LACK THE WILL to see things as they really are, there is nothing so mystifying as the obvious. This is the case, I think, with the new upsurge of radicalism that is now shaking much of Western society to its foundations. We have constructed the most ingenious sociological and psychological theories—as well as a few disingenuously naïve ones— to explain this phenomenon. But there is in truth no mystery here. Our youthful rebels are anything but inarticulate; and though they utter a great deal of nonsense, the import of what they are saying is clear enough. What they are saying is that they dislike—to put it mildly—the liberal, individualist, capitalist civilization that stands ready to receive them as citizens. They are rejecting this offer of citizenship and are declaring their desire to see some other kind of civilization replace it.

That most of them do not always put the matter as explicitly or as candidly as this is beside the point. Some of them do, of course; we try to dismiss them as "the lunatic fringe." But the mass of dissident young are not, after all, sufficiently educated to understand the implications of everything they say. Besides, it is so much easier for the less bold among them to insist that what they find outrageous are the defects and shortcomings of the present system. Such shortcomings undeniably exist and are easy polemical marks. And, at the other end, it is so much easier for the adult generations to accept such polemics as representing the sum and substance of their dissatisfaction. It is consoling to think that the turmoil among them is provoked by the extent to which our society falls short of realizing its ideals. But the plain truth is that it is these ideals themselves that are being rejected. Our young radicals are far less dismayed at America's failure to become what it ought to be than they are contemptuous of what it thinks it ought to be. For them, as for Oscar Wilde, it is not the average American who is disgusting; it is the ideal American.

This is why one can make so little impression on them with arguments about how much progress has been made in the past decades, or is being made today, toward racial equality, or abolishing poverty, or fighting pollution, or whatever it is that we conventionally take as a sign of "progress." The obstinacy with which they remain deaf to such "liberal" arguments is not all perverse or irrational, as some would like to think. It arises, rather, out of a perfectly sincere, if often inchoate, animus against the American system itself. This animus stands for a commitment—*to* what remains to be seen, but *against* what is already only too evident.

Dissatisfaction with the liberal-capitalist ideal, as distinct from indignation at failures to realize this ideal, are coterminous with the history of capitalism itself. Indeed, the cultural history of the capitalist epoch is not much more than a record of the varying ways such dissatisfaction could be expressed—in poetry, in the novel, in drama, in painting, and today even in the movies. Nor, again, is there any great mystery why, from the first stirrings of the romantic movement, poets and philosophers have never had much regard for the capitalist civilization in which they lived and worked. But to understand this fully, one must be able to step outside the "progressive" ideology which makes us assume that liberal capitalism is the "natural" state of man toward which humanity has always aspired. There is nothing more natural about capitalist civilization than about many others that have had, or will have, their day. Capitalism represents a sum of human choices about the good life and the good society. These choices inevitably have their associated costs, and after two hundred years the conviction seems to be spreading that the costs have got out of line.

What did capitalism promise? First of all, it promised continued improvement in the material conditions of all its citizens, a promise without precedent in human history. Secondly, it promised an equally unprecedented measure of individual freedom for all these same citizens. And lastly, it held out the promise that, amidst this prosperity and liberty, the individual could satisfy his instinct for self-perfection—for leading a virtuous life that satisfied the demands of his spirit (or, as one used to say, his soul)—and that the free exercise of such individual virtue would aggregrate into a just society.

Now, it is important to realize that though these aims were in one sense more ambitious than any previously set forth by a political ideology, in another sense they were far more modest. Whereas, as Joseph Cropsey has pointed out, Adam Smith defined "prudence" democratically as "the care of the health, of the fortune, of the rank of the individual," Aristotle had defined that term aristocratically, to mean "the quality of mind concerned with things just and noble and good for man." By this standard, all pre-capitalist systems had been, to one degree or another, Aristotelian: they were interested in creating a high and memorable civilization even if this were shared only by a tiny minority. In contrast, capitalism lowered its sights, but offered its shares in bourgeois civilization to the entire citizenry. Tocqueville, as usual, astutely caught this difference between the aristocratic civilizations of the past and the new liberal capitalism he saw emerging in the United States:

> In aristocratic societies the class that gives the tone to opinion and has the guidance of affairs, being permanently and hereditarily placed above the multitude, naturally conceives a lofty idea of itself and man. It loves to invent for him noble pleasures, to carve out splendid objects for his ambition. Aristocracies often commit very tyrannical and inhuman actions, but they rarely entertain groveling thoughts. . . .
>
> [In democracies, in contrast] there is little energy of character but customs are mild and laws humane. If there are few instances of exalted heroism or of virtues of the highest, brightest, and purest temper, men's habits are regular, violence is rare, and cruelty almost unknown. . . . Genius becomes rare, information more diffused. . . . There is less perfection, but more abundance, in all the productions of the arts.

It is because "high culture" inevitably has an aristocratic bias —it would not be "high" if it did not—that, from the beginnings of the capitalist era, it has always felt contempt for the bourgeois mode of existence. That mode of existence purposively depreciated the very issues that were its *raison d'être*. It did so by making them, as no society had ever dared or desired to do, matters of personal taste, according to the prescription of Adam Smith in his *Theory of Moral Sentiments:*

> Though you despise that picture, or that poem, or even that system of philosophy, which I admire, there is little danger of our quarreling upon that account. Neither of us can reasonably be

much interested about them. They ought all of them to be matters of great indifference to us both; so that, though our opinions may be opposite, our affections shall be very nearly the same.

In short, an amiable philistinism was inherent in bourgeois society, and this was bound to place its artists and intellectuals in an antagonistic posture toward it. This antagonism was irrepressible—the bourgeois world could not suppress it without violating its own liberal creed; the artists could not refrain from expressing their hostility without denying their most authentic selves. But the conflict could, and was, contained so long as capitalist civilization delivered on its three basic promises. It was only when the third promise, of a virtuous life and a just society, was subverted by the dynamics of capitalism itself, as it strove to fulfill the other two—affluence and liberty —that the bourgeois order came, in the minds of the young especially, to possess a questionable legitimacy.

I can think of no better way of indicating the distance that capitalism has traveled from its original ideological origins than by contrasting the most intelligent defender of capitalism today with his predecessors. I refer to Friederich von Hayek, who has as fine and as powerful a mind as is to be found anywhere, and whose *Constitution of Liberty* is one of the most thoughtful works of the last decades. In that book, he offers the following argument against viewing capitalism as a system that incarnates any idea of justice:

Most people will object not to the bare fact of inequality but to the fact that the differences in reward do not correspond to any recognizable differences in the merit of those who receive them. The answer commonly given to this is that a free society on the whole achieves this kind of justice. This, however, is an indefensible contention if by justice is meant proportionality of reward to moral merit. Any attempt to found the case for freedom on this argument is very damaging to it, since it concedes that material rewards ought to be made to correspond to recognizable merit and then opposes the conclusion that most people will draw from this by an assertion which is untrue. The proper answer is that in a free society it is neither desirable nor practicable that material rewards should be made generally to correspond to what men recognize as merit and that it is an essential characteristic of a free society that an individual's position should not necessarily depend on the views that his fellows hold about the merit he has acquired. . . . A society in which the position of the individual was made to correspond to human ideas of moral merit would therefore be the exact opposite of a free society. It would be a society in which people were rewarded for duty performed instead of for success. . . . But if nobody's knowledge is sufficient to guide all human action, there is also no human being who is competent to reward all efforts according to merit.

This argument is admirable both for its utter candor and for its firm opposition to all those modern authoritarian ideologies, whether rationalist or irrationalist, which give a self-selected elite the right to shape men's lives and fix their destinies according to its preconceived notions of good and evil, merit and demerit. But it is interesting to note what Hayek is doing: he is opposing a *free* society to a *just* society—because, he says, while we know what freedom is, we have no generally accepted knowledge of what justice is. Elsewhere he writes:

Since they [i.e., differentials in wealth and income] are not the effect of anyone's design or intentions, it is meaningless to describe the manner in which the market distributed the good things of this world among particular people as just or unjust. . . . No test or criteria have been found or can be found by which such rules of "social justice" can be assessed. . . . They would have to be determined by the arbitrary will of the holders of power.

Now, it may be that this is the best possible defense that can be made of a free society. But if this is the case, one can fairly say that "capitalism" is (or was) one thing, and a "free society" another. For capitalism, during the first hundred years or so of its existence, did lay claim to being a just social order, in the meaning later given to that concept by Paul Elmer More: "Such a distribution of power and privilege, and of property as the symbol and instrument of these, as at once will satisfy the distinctions of reason among the superior, and will not outrage the feelings of the inferior." As a matter of fact, capitalism at its apogee saw itself as the most just social order the world has ever witnessed, because it replaced all arbitrary (e.g., inherited) distributions of power, privilege, and property with a distribution that was directly and intimately linked to personal merit—this latter term being inclusive of both personal abilities and personal virtues.

Writing shortly before the Civil War, George Fitzhugh, the most gifted of Southern apologists for slavery, attacked the capitalist North in these terms:

In a free society none but the selfish virtues are in repute, because none other help a man in the race of competition. In such a society virtue loses all her loveliness, because of her selfish aims. Good men and bad men have the same end in view—self-promotion and self-elevation. . . .

At the time, the accusation was a half-truth. The North was not yet "a free society," in Hayek's sense or Fitzhugh's. It was still in good measure a bourgeois society in which the capitalist mode of existence involved moral self-discipline and had a visible aura of spiritual grace. It was a society in which "success" was indeed seen as having what Hayek has said it ought never to have: a firm connection with "duty performed." It was a society in which Theodore Parker could write of a leading merchant: "He had no uncommon culture of the understanding or the imagination, and of the higher reason still less. But in respect of the *greater faculties*—in respect of conscience, affection, the religious element—he was well born, well bred." In short, it was a society still permeated by the

Puritan ethic, the Protestant ethic, the capitalist ethic—call it what you will. It was a society in which it was agreed that there was a strong correlation between certain personal virtues—frugality, industry, sobriety, reliability, piety—and the way in which power, privilege, and property were distributed. And this correlation was taken to be the sign of a just society, not merely of a free one. Samuel Smiles or Horatio Alger would have regarded Professor Hayek's writings as slanderous of his fellow Christians, blasphemous of God, and ultimately subversive of the social order. I am not sure about the first two of these accusations, but I am fairly certain of the validity of the last.

This is not the place to recount the history and eventual degradation of the capitalist ethic in America. Suffice it to say that, with every passing decade, Fitzhugh's charge, that "virtue loses all her loveliness, because of her selfish aims," became more valid. From having been a *capitalist, republican community*, with shared values and a quite unambiguous claim to the title of a just order, the United States became a *free, democratic society* where the will to success and privilege was severed from its moral moorings.

But can men live in a free society if they have no reason to believe it is also a just society? I do not think so. My reading of history is that, in the same way as men cannot for long tolerate a sense of spiritual meaninglessness in their individual lives, so they cannot for long accept a society in which power, privilege, and property are not distributed according to some morally meaningful criteria. Nor is equality itself any more acceptable than inequality—neither is more "natural" than the other—if equality is merely a brute fact rather than a consequence of an ideology or social philosophy. This explains what otherwise seems paradoxical: that small inequalities in capitalist countries can become the source of intense controversy while relatively larger inequalities in socialist or communist countries are blandly overlooked. Thus, those same young radicals who are infuriated by trivial inequalities in the American economic system are quite blind to grosser inequalities in the Cuban system. This is usually taken as evidence of hypocrisy or self-deception. I would say it shows, rather, that people's notions of equality or inequality have extraordinarily little to do with arithmetic and almost everything to do with political philosophy.

I believe that what holds for equality also holds for liberty. People feel free when they subscribe to a prevailing social philosophy; they feel unfree when the prevailing social philosophy is unpersuasive; and the existence of constitutions or laws or judiciaries have precious little to do with these basic feelings. The average working man in nineteenth-century America had far fewer "rights" than his counterpart today; but he was far more likely to boast about his being a free man.

So I conclude, despite Professor Hayek's ingenious analysis, that men cannot accept the historical accidents of the marketplace—seen merely as accidents—as the basis for an enduring and legitimate entitlement to power, privilege, and property. And, in actual fact, Professor Hayek's rationale for modern capitalism is never used outside a small academic enclave; I even suspect it cannot be believed except by those whose minds have been shaped by overlong exposure to scholasticism. Instead, the arguments offered to justify the social structure of capitalism now fall into three main categories:

1) *The Protestant Ethic.* This, however, is now reserved for the lower socioeconomic levels. It is still believed, and it is still reasonable to believe, that worldly success among the working class, lower-middle class, and even middle class has a definite

connection with personal virtues such as diligence, rectitude, sobriety, honest ambition, etc., etc. And, so far as I can see, the connection is not only credible but demonstrable. It does seem that the traditional bourgeois virtues are efficacious among these classes—at least, it is rare to find successful men in these classes who do not to a significant degree exemplify them. But no one seriously claims that these traditional virtues will open the corridors of corporate power to anyone, or that the men who now occupy the executive suites are— or even aspire to be—models of bourgeois virtue.

2) *The Darwinian Ethic.* This is to be found mainly among small businessmen who are fond of thinking that their "making it" is to be explained as "the survival of the fittest." They are frequently quite right, of course, in believing the metaphor appropriate to their condition and to the ways in which they achieved it. But it is preposterous to think that the mass of men will ever accept as legitimate a social order formed in accordance with the laws of the jungle. Men may be animals, but they are political animals—and, what comes to not such a different thing, moral animals too. The fact that for several decades after the Civil War, the Darwinian ethic, as popularized by Herbert Spencer, could be taken seriously by so many social theorists represents one of the most bizarre and sordid episodes in American intellectual history. It could not last; and did not.

3) *The Technocratic Ethic.* This is the most prevalent justification of corporate capitalism today, and finds expression in an insistence on "performance." Those who occupy the seats of corporate power, and enjoy the prerogatives and privileges thereof, are said to acquire legitimacy by their superior ability to achieve superior "performance"—in economic growth, managerial efficiency, technological innovation. In a sense, what is claimed is that these men are accomplishing social tasks, and fulfilling social responsibilities, in an especially efficacious way.

There are, however, two fatal flaws in this argument. First, if one defines "'performance" in a strictly limited and measurable sense, then one is applying a test that any ruling class is bound, on fairly frequent occasions, to fail. Life has its ups and downs; so do history and economics; and men who can only claim legitimacy *via* performance are going to have to spend an awful lot of time and energy explaining why things are not going as well as they ought to. Such repeated, defensive apologias, in the end, will be hollow and unconvincing. Indeed, the very concept of "legitimacy," in its historical usages, is supposed to take account of and make allowances for all those rough passages a society will have to navigate. If the landed gentry of Britain during those centuries of its dominance, or the business class in the United States during the first century and a half of our national history, had insisted that it be judged by performance alone, it would have flunked out of history. So would every other ruling class that ever existed.

Second, if one tries to avoid this dilemma by giving the term "performance" a broader and larger meaning, then one inevitably finds oneself passing beyond the boundaries of bourgeois propriety. It is one thing to say with Samuel Johnson that men honestly engaged in business are doing the least mischief that men are capable of; it is quite another thing to assert that they are doing the greatest good—this is only too patently untrue. For the achievement of the greatest good, more than successful performance in business is necessary. Witness how vulnerable our corporate managers are to accusations that they are befouling our environment. What these accusations really add up to is the statement that the business system in the United States does not create a beautiful, refined, gracious, and tranquil civilization. To which our corporate leaders are replying: "Oh, we can perform that mission too—just give us time." But there is no good reason to think they can accomplish this noncapitalist mission; nor is there any reason to believe that they have any proper entitlement even to try.

It is, I think, because of the decline of the bourgeois ethic, and the consequent drainage of legitimacy out of the business system, that the issue of "participation" has emerged with such urgency during these past years. It is a common error to take this word at its face value—to assume that, in our organized and bureaucratized society, the average person is more isolated, alienated, or powerless than ever before, and that the proper remedy is to open new avenues of "participation." We are then perplexed when, the avenues having been open, we find so little traffic passing through. We give college students the right to representation on all sorts of committees—and then discover they never bother to come to meetings. We create new popularly elected "community" organizations in the ghettos—and then discover that ghetto residents won't come out to vote. We decentralize New York City's school system—only to discover that the populace is singularly uninterested in local school board elections.

I doubt very much that the average American is actually more isolated or powerless today than in the past. The few serious studies that have been made on this subject indicate that we have highly romanticized notions of the past—of the degree to which ordinary people were ever involved in community activities—and highly apocalyptic notions of the present. If one takes membership in civic-minded organizations as a criterion, people are unquestionably more "involved" today than ever before in our history. Maybe that's not such a good criterion, but it is a revealing aspect of this whole problem that those who make large statements on this matter rarely give us any workable or testable criteria at all.

But I would not deny that more people, even if more specifically "involved" than ever before, also feel more "alienated" in a general way. And this, I would suggest, is because the institutions of our society have lost their vital connection with the values which are supposed to govern the private lives of our citizenry. They no longer exemplify these values; they no longer magnify them; they no longer reassuringly sustain them. When it is said that the institutions of our society have become appallingly "impersonal," I take this to mean that they have lost any shape that is congruent with the private moral codes which presumably govern individual life. (That presumption, of course, may be factually weak, but it is nonetheless efficacious as long as people hold it.) The "outside" of our social life has ceased being harmonious with the "inside"—the mode of distribution of power, privilege, and property, and hence the very principle of authority, no longer "makes sense" to the bewildered citizen. And when institutions cease to "make sense" in this way, all the familiar criteria of success or failure become utterly irrelevant.

As I see it, then, the demand for "participation" is best appreciated as a demand for authority—for leadership that holds the promise of reconciling the inner and outer worlds of the citizen. So far from its being a hopeful reawakening of the democratic spirit, it signifies a hunger for authority that leads toward some kind of plebiscitary democracy at best, and is in any case not easy to reconcile with liberal democracy as we traditionally have known it. I find it instructive that such old-fashioned populists as Hubert Humphrey and Edmund Muskie, whose notions of "participation" are both liberal and traditional, fail to catch the imagination of our dissidents in the way that Robert Kennedy did. The late Senator Kennedy was very much a leader—one can imagine Humphrey or Muskie participating in an old-fashioned town meeting, one can only envision Kennedy dominating a town rally. One can also envision those who "participated" in such a rally feeling that they had achieved a kind of "representation" previously denied them.

For a system of liberal, representative government to work, free elections are not enough. The results of the political process and of the exercise of individual freedom—the distribution of power, privilege, and property—must also be seen as in some profound sense expressive of the values that govern the lives of individuals. An idea of self-government, if it is to be viable, must encompass both the private and the public sectors. If it does not—if the principles that organize public life seem to have little relation to those that shape private lives—you have "alienation," and *anomie*, and a melting away of established principles of authority.

Milton Friedman, arguing in favor of Hayek's extreme libertarian position, has written that the free man "recognizes no national purpose except as it is the consensus of the purposes for which the citizens severally strive." If he is using the term "consensus" seriously, then he must be assuming that there is a strong homogeneity of values among the citizenry, and that these values give a certain corresponding shape to the various institutions of society, political and economic. Were that the case, then it is indeed true that a "national purpose" arises automatically and organically out of the social order itself. Something like this did happen when liberal capitalism was in its prime, vigorous and self-confident. But is that our condition today? I think not—just as I think Friedman doesn't really mean "consensus" but rather the mere aggregation of selfish aims. In such a blind and accidental arithmetic, the sum floats free from the addenda, and its legitimacy is infinitely questionable.

The inner spiritual chaos of the times, so powerfully created by the dynamics of capitalism itself, is such as to make nihilism an easy temptation. A "free society" in Hayek's sense gives birth in massive numbers to "free spirits"—emptied of moral substance but still driven by primordial moral aspirations. Such people are capable of the most irrational actions. Indeed, it is my impression that under the strain of modern life whole classes of population—and the educated classes most of all—are entering what can only be called, in the strictly clinical sense, a phase of infantile regression. With every passing year, public discourse becomes sillier and more petulant, while human emotions become, apparently, more ungovernable. Some of our most intelligent university professors are now loudly saying things that, had they been uttered by one of their students twenty years ago, would have called forth gentle and urbane reproof.

And yet, if the situation of liberal capitalism today seems so precarious, it is likely nevertheless to survive for a long while, if only because the modern era has failed to come up with any plausible alternatives. Socialism, communism, and fascism have all turned out to be either utopian illusions or sordid frauds. So we shall have time—though not an endless amount of it, for we have already wasted a great deal. We are today in a situation not very different from that described by Herbert Croly in *The Promise of American Life* (1912):

The substance of our national Promise has consisted . . . of an improving popular economic condition, guaranteed by democratic political institutions, and resulting in moral and social amelioration. These manifold benefits were to be obtained merely by liberating the enlightened self-enterprise of the American people. . . . The fulfillment of the American Promise was considered inevitable because it was based upon a combination of self-interest and the natural goodness of human nature. On the other hand, if the fulfillment of our national Promise can no longer be considered inevitable, if it must be considered as equivalent to a conscious national purpose instead of an inexorable national destiny, the implication necessarily is that the trust reposed in individual self-interest has been in some measure betrayed. No pre-established harmony can then exist between the free and abundant satisfaction of private needs and the accomplishment of a morally and socially desirable result.

Croly is not much read these days. He was a liberal reformer with essentially conservative goals. So was Matthew Arnold, fifty years earlier—and he isn't much read these days, either. Neither of them can pass into the conventional anthologies of liberal or conservative thought. I think this is a sad commentary on the ideological barrenness of the liberal and conservative creeds. I also think it is a great pity. For if our private and public worlds are ever again, in our lifetimes, to have a congenial relationship—if virtue is to regain her lost loveliness —then some such combination of the reforming spirit with the conservative ideal seems to me to be what is most desperately wanted.

I use the word "conservative" advisedly. Though the discontents of our civilization express themselves in the rhetoric of "liberation" and "equality," one can detect beneath the surface an acute yearning for order and stability—but a legitimate order, of course, and a legitimized stability. In this connection, I find the increasing skepticism as to the benefits of economic growth and technological innovation suggestive. Such skepticism has been characteristic of conservative critics of liberal capitalism since the beginning of the nineteenth century. One finds it in Coleridge, Carlyle, and Newman—in all those who found it impossible to acquiesce in a "progressive" notion of human history or social evolution. Our dissidents today may think they are exceedingly progressive, but no one who puts greater emphasis on "the quality of life" than on "mere" material enrichment can properly be placed in that category. For the idea of progress in the modern era has always signified that the quality of life would inevitably be improved by material enrichment. To doubt this is to doubt the political metaphysics of modernity and to start the long trek back to pre-modern political philosophy—Plato, Aristotle, Thomas Aquinas, Hooker, Calvin, etc. It seems to me that this trip is quite necessary. Perhaps there we shall discover some of those elements that are most desperately needed by the spiritually impoverished civilization that we have constructed on what once seemed to be sturdy bourgeois foundations.

7

Toward a Restructuring of the University

I HAVE THE GRAVEST DOUBTS that very much of substance will come out of all the current agitation for a "restructuring" of the university. There are a great many reasons why
this is so, among them the fact that practically no one any
longer has a clear notion of what a university is supposed to be,
or do, or mean. We are, all of us, equally vague as to what
the term "higher education" signifies, or what functions and
purposes are properly included in the categories of "student"
or "professor." But, in addition to such basic problems, there
is a simple and proximate obstacle: all the groups—professors,
administrators, and students—now engaged in this enterprise of
"restructuring" are deficient in the will to do anything, or the
power to do anything, or ideas about what might be done.

Let us begin with the faculty, since they are indeed, as they
claim ("Sir, the faculty *is* the university"), the preponderant
estate of this realm. In most universities, it is the faculty that
controls the educational functions and defines the educational
purposes of the institution. It is the faculty that usually ar-
ranges the curriculum, makes staff appointments, etc. It is the
faculty that has the moral authority, the mental capacity, and
a sufficiently intimate knowledge of the realities of the educa-

tional system to operate upon it. Unfortunately, these virtues are far outweighed by an all too human defect—a limited imagination which leads to a lack of objective insight into its own position. What faculty members of our universities fail to see is that any meaningful restructuring will not only have to be done *by* the faculty, but will also have to be done *to* the faculty. And to ask the American professoriat to restructure itself is as sensible as if one had asked Marie Antoinette to establish a republican government in France. Whether or not it coincided with her long-term interests was immaterial; the poor woman couldn't even conceive of the possibility.

Now, I don't mean to suggest that there is anything especially shortsighted or selfish about the American professor. Some of my best friends are professors, and I can testify that they are every bit as broadminded, every bit as capable of disinterested action as the average business executive or higher civil servant. Nor are they particularly smug and complacent. On the contrary, they are all keenly aware of the crisis that has befallen them, while many have long been discontented with their lot and full of haunting insecurities. Nevertheless, they do have one peculiar and notable flaw: being generally liberal and reformist in their political predisposition, they believe themselves able to have a truly liberal and reformist perspective on themselves. This is, of course, an idle fancy. No social group really possesses the imaginative capacity to have a liberal and reformist perspective on itself; individual members of the group may and do—but the group as a whole cannot. Otherwise the history of human society would be what it is not: an amiable progression of thoughtful self-reformations by classes and institutions.

So the beginning of wisdom, in thinking about our universities, is to assume that the professors are a class with a vested interest in, and an implicit ideological commitment to, the *status quo* broadly defined, and that reform will have to be imposed upon them as upon everyone else. If any empirical proof were required of the validity of these assumptions, one need only cast a glance over the various proposals for university reform that have been made by faculty committees at Berkeley and elsewhere. These proposals have one distinguishing characteristic: at no point, and in no way, do they cost the faculty anything—not money, not time, not power over their conditions of employment. They liberally impose inconveniences upon the administration, upon the taxpayers, upon the secondary schools, upon the community. But they never inconvenience the faculty. They never, for instance, increase its teaching load. (On the contrary: after many years of "restructuring" at Berkeley, professors there now spend *less* time in the classroom than they used to.) They never suggest anything that would intrude on those four-month vacations; they never interfere with such off-campus activities as consultancies, the writing of textbooks, traveling fellowships, etc.; they never discourage the expensive—but convenient—proliferation of courses in their specialized areas; they never even make attendance at committee meetings compulsory. This is precisely what one would expect when one asks a privileged class to reform the institution which is its very *raison d'être*. It is rather like asking corporation executives or trade-union leaders or officials of a government agency, all of whom have been given lifelong tenure in their present positions, to "restructure" the institutions and redefine their positions.

I have touched upon this question of tenure because of its symbolic significance. Few professors, in conversation, will defend the present tenure system, whereby senior and middle-level faculty are given a personal, lifelong monopoly on their positions. They will accept the criticisms of it by Robert Nisbet and others as largely valid. They will concede that it could be substantially modified—via long-term contracts, generous severance agreements, etc.—without any danger to academic freedom and with obvious benefits to everyone. They will agree that the "controversial" professor, whom tenure was supposed to protect, is today in great demand and short supply, whereas the mediocre professor is its prime beneficiary. They may even admit that the presence of a tenured faculty is one of the reasons that the university has been—with the possible exception of the post office—the least inventive (or even adaptive) of our social institutions since the end of World War II. They will allow that tenure in the university, like seniority in a craft union, makes for all sorts of counterproductive rigidities. But they will then go on to dismiss the whole issue as utterly "academic." To tamper with tenure, they argue, would produce fits and convulsions throughout their well-ordered universe. Nothing can or will be done, and they themselves could not be counted on to try. Even those economists who argue in favor of a free market for labor everywhere else somehow never think of applying this doctrine to themselves.

So when these same people announce that, to cope with the crisis in the university, they are going to "restructure" the institution, one has the right to be skeptical. To suppose that they actually will do any such thing is probably the most "academic" idea of all.

II

Nor is the administration going to "restructure" the university. It couldn't do it if it tried; and it is not going to try because it doesn't regard itself as competent even to think about the problem. University administration in the United States today

combines relative powerlessness with near-absolute mindlessness on the subject of education.

That statement about powerlessness needs to be qualified in
one respect. Though a great many people are under the impression that the boards of trustees are the "real" power structure of the university, this is in fact the one group over which
the administration does wield considerable influence. The
trustees of a modern university are rather like the boards of di-
rectors of a modern corporation. They represent a kind of
"stand-by" authority, ready to take over if the executive of-
ficers lead the organization into a scandalous mess. (Having
little firsthand knowledge of educational institutions, they will
then usually make the mess even worse than it was; but that's
another story.) They also may—repeat: *may*—intervene in
certain broad economic decisions, such as the construction of a
new campus, the launching of a major fund-raising drive, etc.
But on the whole, and in the ordinary course of events, they
solemnly rubber-stamp whatever the administration has done
or proposes to do.

And that's about the sum and substance of "administrative
power." True, a determined administration can badger and
bribe and blackmail the faculty into marginal revisions of the
curriculum, just as a determined administration can have some
influence over senior appointments. But most administrations
are not all that determined—like everyone else, university administrators prefer an untroubled life. And even where they
are determined, it doesn't make all that much difference, from
an outsider's point of view. Within the institution, of course,
even small differences can cause great anguish and excitement.

As for the administration's power over students, that hardly
seems worth discussing at a time when the issue being debated
is the students' power over the administration. Suffice it to say
that where disciplinary power does exist on paper, it is rarely

used; and it is now in the process of ceasing to exist even on paper.* In this respect, university administrators are ironically very much *in loco parentis*. They have about as much control over their nineteen- and twenty-year-old charges as the parents do.

There might be something to deplore in this situation if one had reason to think that university administrators could wisely use power, if they had it. But there is no such reason, if what we are interested in is higher education. University administrators have long since ceased to have anything to say about education. By general consent, their job is administration, not education. When was the last time a university president came forth with a new idea about education? When was the last time a university president wrote a significant book about the education of—as distinct from the government of—"his" students? Robert M. Hutchins was the last of that breed; he has had no noteworthy successors. Indeed, the surest way for an ambitious man never to become a university president is to let it be known that he actually has a philosophy of education. The faculty, suspicious of possible interference, will rise up in rebellion.

The university president today is primarily the chief executive of a corporate institution, not an educator. Unfortunately, he usually is also a poor executive, for various reasons. To begin with, he is almost invariably a professor, with no demonstrated managerial experience. More important, there are few meaningful standards against which to judge his performance, as distinct from his popularity. Since most university administrators have no clear idea of what they are supposed to

* "Colleges are not churches, clinics, or even parents. Whether or not a student burns a draft card, participates in a civil-rights march, engages in premarital or extramarital sexual activity, becomes pregnant, attends church, sleeps all day or drinks all night, is not really the concern of an educational institution."—The president of the American Association for Higher Education as reported in *Time*, July 11, 1968.

be doing, they end up furiously imitating one another, on
the assumption—doubtless correct—that to be immune from
invidious comparisons is to be largely exempt from criticism.
Thus, at the moment, all administrations are proudly ex-
panding the size of their plant, their facilities, and their student
bodies. An outsider might wonder: Why should any single
institution feel that it has to train scholars in all disciplines?
Why can't there be a division of labor among the graduate
schools? Aren't our universities perhaps too big already? Such
questions are occasionally raised at conferences of educators—
but, since every administrator has no other criterion for "success" than the quantitative increase in students, faculty, campus
grounds, etc., these questions spark no debate at all.

As a matter of fact, university administrators never get
much criticism—though, of course, they are convenient scape-
goats who are instantly *blamed* for anything that goes wrong.
It is interesting to note that, despite the fact that our best
economists are all professors, there has been little public
criticism from them on the grotesquely conservative way in
which universities invest their endowment funds. It was not
until the Ford Foundation's McGeorge Bundy made an issue of
it that the universities began to bestir themselves. Similarly, it
was an off-campus man, Beardsley Ruml, who, some fifteen
years ago, pointed out that it was wasteful to leave campus
facilities unused for months at a time because of the vacation
schedule. One would have thought that this idea could have
passed through the minds of professors of management, or
city planning, or something.

An interesting instance of the charmed life of university administrators is a recent report of the Carnegie Commission on
the Future of Higher Education. Written by an economist,
it delicately refuses to raise any interesting questions and limits
itself to arguing for the need of ever greater government

subsidies. After pointing out that the deficit in university budgets is largely incurred by the graduate divisions—a graduate student costs about three or four times as much as an undergraduate—the Carnegie report offers by way of explanation of the costliness of graduate education the following: "The conscientious supervision of a student's independent work is the essence of high-level graduate education. . . ."

What this means in practice, as everyone knows, is that the only way a university can attract big faculty names away from other places is by offering them minimal teaching loads in the graduate division, and the only way it can attract the brightest graduate students away from other schools is by offering them attractive (i.e., expensive) fellowships. Whether or not it makes sense for each institution of higher learning to adopt such a competitive policy would seem to be an important problem; but the Carnegie Commission loyally refrained from exploring it. Nor did it show any interest in whether in fact there is "conscientious supervision" in graduate schools, and if so how extensive or effective it is. From casual conversation with graduate students, one gets the impression that such supervision is not all that common, to put it mildly.

In short and in sum: university administrations have neither the power, nor the inclination, nor the stimulus of informed criticism which would result in any serious efforts at "restructuring" their institutions.

III

And the students? They, alas, are indeed for the most part rebels without a cause—and without a hope of accomplishing anything except mischief and ruin.

In our society and in our culture, with its pathetic belief in progress and its grotesque accent on youth, it is almost impossible to speak candidly about the students. Thus, though most thoughtful people will condemn the "excesses" committed by rebellious students, they will in the same breath pay tribute to their "idealism" and their sense of "commitment." I find this sort of cant to be preposterous and disgusting. It seems to me that a professor whose students have spat at him and called him a "motherfucker" (it happened at Columbia) ought to be moved to more serious and more manly reflection on what his students are really like, as against what popular mythology says they are supposed to be like.

My own view is that a significant minority of today's student body obviously consists of a mob who have no real interest in higher education or in the life of the mind, and whose passions are inflamed by a debased popular culture that prevails unchallenged on the campus. We are reluctant to believe this because so many of the young people who constitute this mob have high IQs and received good academic grades in high school, and because their popular culture is chic rather than philistine in an old-fashioned way. Which is to say: we are reluctant to believe that youngsters of a certain social class, assembled on the grounds of an educational institution, can be a "mob" in the authentic sociological sense of that term. (We are also reluctant to believe it because many of these students are our children, and we love them regardless of what they do. Such love is, of course, natural and proper. On the other hand, it is worth reminding oneself that members of lower-class lynch mobs have loving fathers and mothers too.)

The really interesting question is: How did they get that way? After all, we do assume that young people of a certain intelligence, provided with a decent education, will be more rational—and therefore more immune to mob instincts—as they near the end of their education than they were at the beginning. The assumption is plausible; but it also patently fails to hold in many instances, and this can only represent a terrible judgment on our system of education.

How is it possible for a Columbia or Berkeley sophomore, junior, or even graduate student to believe in the kinds of absurd simplicities they mouth at their rallies—especially when, before entering college, many of these youngsters would have been quick to recognize them as nothing but absurd simplicities? How is it possible for a radical university student—and there is no reason why a university student shouldn't be radical—to take Che Guevara or Chairman Mao seriously when, in his various courses, he is supposed to have read Marx, Max Weber, Tocqueville, has been examined on them, and has passed the examination?

When I discuss this problem with my professor friends, I am informed that I display a naïve faith in the power of formal instruction as against the force of the *Zeitgeist*. And there is a measure of justice in this rejoinder. There can be no doubt that we are witnessing, all over the world, a kind of generational spasm—a sociological convulsion whose roots must go deep and far back and must involve the totality of our culture rather than merely the educational parts of it. It is fairly clear, for example, that many of the students are actually revolting against the bourgeois social and moral order as a whole, and are merely using the university as a convenient point of departure. Whether their contempt for this order is justified is a topic worthy of serious discussion—which, curiously enough, it hardly ever receives in the university. But, in any case, this question ought not to distract us from the fact that those radical students who are most vociferous about the iniquities of the university are the least interested in any productive "restructuring."

On the other hand, not all the rebellious students are all that radical politically; and it does seem to me that, in these cases, it ought to be possible for a university education to countervail against the mish-mash of half-baked and semiliterate ideologies that so many students so effortlessly absorb within a few months of arriving on campus. My own opinion, for what it's worth, is that the college and the university fail to educate their students because they have long since ceased trying to do so.

The university has become very good at training its students for the various professions; and it is noteworthy that, within the university, the professional schools and divisions have been the least turbulent. But for the ordinary college student—majoring in the humanities or in the social sciences—the university has become little more than an elegant "pad," with bull sessions that have course numbers or with mass lectures that mumble into one ear and ramble out the other.*

The entire conception of a liberal education—of the most serious ideas of our civilization being taught by professors who took them seriously—has disappeared, under pressure of one kind or another. The graduate divisions, with their insistence on pre-professional training, have done their part; but so has the whole temper of our educational system over the past decades, with its skepticism toward "great ideas" in general and toward great ideas of the past in particular. I believe that, when students demand that their studies be "relevant," this is what they are unwittingly demanding. After all, what could be more "relevant" today than the idea of "political obligation"—a central theme in the history of Western political philosophy—or the meaning of "justice"? And, in fact, on the few campuses where such teaching still exists, the students do find it "relevant," and exciting and illuminating.

---

* A special word is necessary about sociology departments, whose students play a leading—perhaps critical—role in the current rebellion. Sociology is an odd kind of hybrid: a profession many of whose members are completely

But, whether I am right or wrong in this appraisal, the whole issue is, like so many others, "academic." The students think they are rebelling against the university as a "bureaucratic" institution, and they think it so powerfully that they are not likely to listen to anyone who informs them that they are really rebelling against a soulless institution—one that has been emptied of its ideal content. So those who are not set upon destroying the university will be permitted to tinker at "restructuring" it. They will serve on committees that define the curriculum; they will help enforce a dwindling minimum of student discipline; they will be solemnly listened to instead of being preached at.

But you can't reform an institution unless you know what you want; and though our university students have always been encouraged to want the true, the good, and the beautiful, they have never been taught how to think about the conditions and consequences of such desires. To date, most of the reforms sponsored by students have been in the direction of removing their obligation to get any kind of education at all. It is not surprising that harassed administrators and preoccupied professors are quick to find such proposals perfectly "reasonable."*

---

unprofessional in outlook, temperament, and intellectual rigor. When I was in New York's City College in the late 1930's, most students majored in sociology because it was the closest thing to a major in current social problems that the curriculum offered—and majoring in such problems was what they really wanted to do. In the end, most of them did become professional sociologists; and if they remained interested in social problems and social reform, their interest was anything but simple-minded. But these days, though the motivation for majoring in sociology is still a heightened concern with social problems, the number of sociology majors is so large, the departments so amorphous, the curriculum so sprawling, that it is quite easy for a student to move through his courses with his passions never being seriously disturbed by a sociological idea.

*Jacques Barzun, in his recently published *The American University*, points out that it has long been common in many universities for students, at the end of a course, to hand in written critiques of its form and substance. He also

IV

So where are we? In an impasse, it would appear. Here we have a major social institution in a flagrant condition of crisis, and not one of the natural social forces involved with this institution can be relied upon to do any of the necessary work of reformation. In situations of this kind, the tradition is for the governmental authorities to step in and fill the power vacuum. And such, I think, will again have to be the case this time.

That last sentence made even me, its author, shudder as it was written. The spectacle of state or federal legislators invading the campus en masse for solemn investigation or deliberation is the kind of tragic farce we can do without. And the idea of state legislators or congressmen trying to impose educational reforms by legislation is as fantastic as it is horrifying. Still, the fact remains that there is a genuine "public interest" at issue here, and there is no one except government who can be asked to defend it. Fortunately, I believe that for once we are in luck, in that the particular circumstances of the moment permit government to act in an indirect, non-coercive, prudent, yet possibly effective way.

The first such particular circumstance is the fact that the very idea of "higher education" has become so devoid of specific meaning that there is little danger of government, or anyone else, imposing some kind of orthodox straitjacket on the prevailing chaos. There just aren't any such orthodoxies available. Indeed, the very reason we have a crisis in the uni-

---

points out that, if one surveys these critiques over a period of time, one discovers that the most recent will be demanding a return to what was rejected by students only a few years back.

versities is because all such traditional notions about the function and ends of higher education have, during these past three decades, become otiose.

The real problem at the moment is that no one—not the faculty, not the administration, not the students—has any kind of clear idea of what any "institution of higher learning" is supposed to be accomplishing. It is even beginning to be suspected by many that such phrases as "the university" or "higher education" have acquired different and contradictory meanings, that the vast number of young people now moving onto the campuses are too diverse in their interests and talents to be contained within the old category of "university students," and that the root cause of our distemper is our failure to sort out all these meanings and people, and to make suitable institutional adjustments.

In other words, the situation seems to be such that what we need is a huge injection of pluralism into an educational system that has, through the working out of natural forces, become homogeneous and meaningless at the same time. No one can presume to say what the future pattern of higher education in America should look like. Not until we have far more experimentation—not until we have tried out different kinds of "universities" for different kinds of "students"—can we even hope to know what the real options are. In the ordinary course of events the prospects for this kind of pluralism would be so dim as to be utopian: none of the existing institutions can be counted on to cooperate except in a ritualistic and rather hypocritical way. But this leads me to the second "particular circumstance," which gives the prospect an honest dimension of reality.

This second particular circumstance is the fact that government—especially the federal government—is going to be pouring more and more money into the universities. This is inevitable, and I am willing to persuade myself that it is desirable. But it is neither inevitable nor desirable that the money should flow through the conventional channels—i.e., directly from the public treasury to the bursar's office. Understandably enough, college presidents cannot imagine it proceeding otherwise—higher education is "their" province, and they feel strongly that the money should be "theirs" to expend as administrative discretion and wisdom prescribe. But the citizens of this republic have a claim to assert that higher education is "their" province, too; and they have a right to insist that public monies must be expended in such a manner as might overcome the crisis in our universities, instead of deepening it.

What I would therefore like to see—and the idea is one that is slowly gaining favor with many observers; it is not original with me—is something along these lines: (a) state expenditures for higher public education should be frozen at the present level, and all increases in this budget should take the form of loans to qualifying students—these loans being valid for out-of-state institutions as well as in-state ones;* (b) federal grants to institutions of higher learning (excepting research grants) should be slowly phased out entirely, and this money—together with new appropriations which are to be expected—should also be replaced by loans to the qualifying student. This means, in brief, that our universities should have a minimum of direct access to public funds to spend as they see fit, since their vision in this matter has turned out to be too imperfect. It also means that students will have more of the only kind of "student

---

* Ideally, the entire state budget for higher education should, in my opinion, take the form of student loans. But so radical a measure has little chance of getting through—the state universities would lobby it to death. Besides, so radical a measure is not really necessary. With a ceiling on their budgets and with inevitably increasing costs, the state universities will be constrained gradually to compete for students in terms of the education they offer, as against the low fees they charge, and their position will become a little less privileged with every passing year.

power" that counts: the freedom to purchase the kind of education they want, on terms acceptable to them.

There are potential benefits and risks attendant on this proposal, and they merit a listing. But, first, one must face the frequently heard objection to student loans—that their repayment may place too great a burden on a student, especially the student from a poor family, after his graduation. This objection can be surmounted. To begin with, not all students would need loans, and many would need only small ones. There are plenty of well-to-do parents who would still want to pay for their children's education. In addition, repayment plans can be—have been—calculated so as to be proportionate to the student's average income during his working life, and to exempt those whose average income would be below a fixed level; and the burden on both student and taxpayer (for a subsidy would still be necessary, especially for women) could be made perfectly tolerable. If one wished to be more egalitarian, one could augment a loan program with a part-scholarship program for those from low-income families. When all is said and done, however, the university graduate is the prime beneficiary, in dollars and cents, of his education; he ought to be the prime taxpayer for it. There is no such thing as "free" higher education. Someone is paying for it and, as things now stand, it is the working class of this country that is paying taxes to send the sons and daughters of the middle class—and of the wealthy, too—through state colleges. (Some 60 per cent of the students at Berkeley come from families with incomes of over $12,000.) It is not an easily defensible state of affairs, though we are now so accustomed to it that it seems the only "natural" one.

Now, as to benefits and risks:

(1) A possible benefit that might realistically be expected is that college students would take a more serious and responsible view of their reasons for being on the campus. To the

extent that they would disrupt their own education, they would be paying for this out of their own pockets. As a consequence, there would certainly be less casual or playful or faddish disruption. One does get the impression that for many students the university is now, like the elementary and high schools, a place of compulsory attendance, and that the occupation of a campus building is a welcome lark and frolic. If these students were called upon to pay for their frolics, some of them at least might go back to swallowing goldfish. This would be bad for the goldfish but good for the rest of us.

(2) Another potential benefit is that the large state universities, denied the subsidy which permits them to set very low tuition rates for state residents, would find it difficult to grow larger than they are; the college population would probably become more widely distributed, with the smaller and medium-sized institutions in a position to attract more students. This would be a good thing. It is clearly foolish to assemble huge and potentially riotous mobs in one place—and to provide them with room, board, a newspaper, and perhaps a radio station to boot. This violates the basic principles of riot control. We should aim at the "scatteration" of the student population, so as to decrease their capacity to cause significant trouble. I would also argue there are likely to be some educational gains from this process.

(3) An obvious risk is that a great many of the radical and dissenting students would use their money to attend newly founded "anti-universities." And many of the black students would veer off into black nationalist institutions of higher learning. Something like this is bound to happen, I suppose, though to what extent is unpredictable. It would, beyond question, create bad publicity for the whole student loan program. On the other hand, it would take the pressure off existing institutions to be both universities and "anti-universities"—as

well as "integrated" and "black nationalist" universities—at the same time. The degree to which such pressure has already been effective would shock parents, state legislators, and public opinion generally were the facts more widely known. Quite a few of our universities have already decided that the only way to avoid on-campus riots is to give students academic credit for off-campus rioting ("field work" in the ghettos, among migrant workers, etc.). And at Harvard—of all places! —there was until recently a course (Social Relations 148) which enrolled several hundred students and was given for credit, whose curriculum was devised by S.D.S., whose classes were taught by S.D.S. sympathizers, and whose avowed aim was "radicalization" of the students.

(4) As a corollary to this last risk, there is the possibility that more new, "good" (in my sense of that term) colleges would also be founded. I'm not too sanguine about this—a fair portion of the academic community would surely look more benevolently on a new college whose curriculum made ample provision for instruction in the theory of guerrilla warfare than one that made a knowledge of classical political philosophy compulsory. Besides, it would be much easier to find "qualified" faculty for the first type than the second. Nevertheless, it is conceivable that the "traditionalists," as well as the academic hipsters, could take advantage of the new state of affairs. And among the students they attract there might be quite a few blacks who are not really interested in studying Swahili or Afro-American culture or "black economics," but who—as things are now moving on the campus—are pretty much forced to do so by their black nationalist fellow students.

(5) The greatest benefit of all, however, is that the new mode of financing higher education will shake things up. Both university administrators and faculty will have to think seri-

ously about the education of the students—and about their own professional integrity as teachers. This shake-up is bound to have both bad and good consequences. Some universities, for instance, will simply try to reckon how they can best pander to what they take to be student sentiment, and many professors will doubtless pay undue attention to their "popularity" among students. On the other hand, it is reasonable to assume that you can't fool all the students—and their parents—all of the time; and if students are paying for their education, most of them will want to be getting their money's worth.

So, at long last, the academic community, and the rest of us as well, will have to engage in sober self-examination, and address ourselves to such questions as: What *is* this "college" of ours, or this "university" of ours? What *is* the "higher education" we offer? What *do* we parents expect from a particular "institution of higher learning" when we send our children there? The answers will certainly be too various to be pleasing to everyone. But at least they will be authentic answers, representing authentic choices.

It would be ridiculous to expect that, during this period of "shake-up," calm will descend upon our campuses. As I have already said, the roots of the student rebellion go very deep, and very far back. I recall Leo Rosten observing long before Columbia that, so far as he could see, what the dissatisfied students were looking for were adults—adults to confront, to oppose, to emulate. It is not going to be easy to satisfy this quest, since our culture for many decades now has been plowing under its adults. But I agree with Rosten that this is what is wanted, and I am certain it will not be achieved until our institutions of higher education reach some kind of common understanding on what kind of adult a young man is ideally supposed to become. This understanding—involving a scrutiny of the values of our civilization—will not come soon or easily, if it ever comes at all. But we must begin to move toward it—and the first step, paradoxically, is to allow a variety of meanings to emerge from our existing, petrified institutions of higher learning.

8

Utopianism and American Politics

L ET US SUPPOSE that we have provided the President
of the United States with two imaginary speeches, both of
which he is dutifully prepared to deliver. They deal, in a
highly general way, with the goals of American foreign policy.
The first speech goes somewhat as follows:

Our American nation, ever since its foundation, has pursued the
ideal of a world without war. This ideal—the abolition of war—has
been the ultimate foundation of our foreign policy, despite all
circumstantial changes of strategy and tactics. The ideal is as
alive today, in our hearts and minds, as it ever was. This Administration is dedicated to pursuing it with the utmost vigor, and
with all the patience and skill that is necessary. We seek, by our
policies, to create a world in which man's inhumanity to man will
become but a horrible memory, in which men will, under the
conditions of a just and secure peace, live harmoniously and crea-
tively together. We seek a world without war, without bloodshed,
without poverty, without oppression or discrimination. Such a
world, I am convinced, is within our reach if only the statesmen
of all nations are sufficiently farsighted to seize the opportunity.
I am confident, moreover, that they will display such farsighted-
ness, and will not let the opportunity for a universal and enduring
peace slip from their grasp. The people of the world—the people
of all nations—demand such a peace. We shall betray their aspira-

tions, and shall certainly be held to account, if we fail to resolve our quarrels and conflicts so as to make man's dream of permanent peace a reality in our own time.

What would happen if the President gave this speech (in a considerably lengthier version, of course)? It is fair to predict —it is indeed absolutely certain—that nothing would happen. It is a perfectly conventional speech, of a kind that many Presidents have given many times. The press corps would yawn over the familiar clichés; the citizenry would scan the headline ("President Reaffirms Goal of World Peace") and then turn to the sports or financial pages; the heads of all nations would formally indicate their approval of these noble sentiments; and "informed sources" in Washington would explain that it is too early to tell what significance, if any, the speech had for any particular area of American foreign policy. As I said: nothing would happen.

Now, let us have the President deliver a rather different speech—our second version. And let it proceed somewhat as follows:

This American nation, ever since its foundation, has for the most part pursued its national interests in a moderate and prudent way. This Administration is determined to continue on this path of moderation and prudence. However, we are well aware that there is no guaranteed path to peace with justice. True, men have always dreamed of perpetual peace, and presumably always will. This dream is a noble one, and a man must be deficient in humanity not to have felt its appeal. But let us remember: It is a dream, whereas we live out our lives in a real and material world that is governed, not by dreams, but by limited possibilities. In this real and material world, conflict between men and war between nations appear to be permanent features of the human condition. It has always been so; we must, if we are to be responsible statesmen, assume that it always will be so. I shall strive to minimize our chances of experiencing war; if war is unavoidable, I shall do my best to limit its extent and the mischief it is bound to create; and whether I am able to limit it or not, I shall always do my utmost to ensure that the war we shall be engaged in will be a just war, and will be justly conducted. I cannot promise you a world without war, for such a promise is inherently fraudulent. But I can promise that we shall conduct our foreign affairs in a responsible and honorable fashion, that we shall make every effort to achieve a reasonable compromise of our differences with other nations, and that whatever calamities befall us will be as little as possible of our own making.

What would happen if the President gave *this* speech? One's imagination is inadequate to the prospect. It is fair to predict, however, that after a shorter or longer period of stunned silence, a storm of censure would gather round the President's head. The press corps would explode with moral indignation, and the headlines this time would be eye-catching ("President Denounces Peace as Impossible Dream"); the citizenry would be alarmed; the heads of all nations would express concern at "the new American belligerency"; only the "informed sources" in Washington would remain steady, explaining that it is too early to tell what significance, if any, the speech had for any particular area of American foreign policy.

And yet—what is wrong with the second speech? I submit that there is nothing wrong with it. It is, in every respect, superior to the meaningless banalities of the first speech. It reads 5,000 years of human experience truthfully and sagaciously, and it announces the results of this reading with a pleasing directness and candor. It is a statesman's speech—whereas the first version was nothing more than a politician's speech. True, it is an American statesman's speech; not everyone would agree that this nation's foreign policy has always displayed such moderation and prudence. But that sort of bias is comprehensible, easily discountable and even justifiable—after all, Presidents of the United States are not supposed to be objective and neutral political philosophers.

So the question arises: If the second speech is so much superior to the first, why is it that no President would ever dare to make it? Why is it that, if the President were to say that no reasonable man can expect enduring peace on earth until the day that our Redeemer cometh, this would be regarded as a terrible, cynical blasphemy—even though it is recognizably one of the most venerable platitudes of the Judaeo-Christian tradition? What is it about our political condition that constrains our leaders to define politics as the pursuit of impossible dreams? Are we the most high-minded people who ever lived, or the most hypocritical?

To that last question, the answer is: If you are extraordinarily high-minded in your political pronouncements, you are bound in the nature of things to be more than ordinarily hypocritical. But it is only in the last half century or so that high-minded hypocrisy has completely driven statesmanlike reasonableness out of the American public forum. The point is important and not at all self-evident to our smog-beclouded eyes, so it is worth a bit of elaboration.

II

The United States has always had, by historical standards, quite ambitious ideological ends of a timeless and universal nature. George Santayana, echoing the worldly wisdom of Old Europe, could dismiss the Declaration of Independence as "a salad of illusions." But these "illusions" represented a deep emotional commitment by a new national community to the idea that government—all government, everywhere—should be subservient to the citizen's individual life, his personal liberty and his pursuit of happiness. True, and inevitably, this fundamental document of the American credo was involved in hypocrisy from the outset: It carefully refrained from saying anything about "the peculiar institution" of slavery which then flourished in this country. Nevertheless, one cannot begin to understand the American people and its history unless one appreciates the extent to which our literature, our journalism, our philosophy, our politics were shaped by this powerful ideological commitment. One does not exaggerate when one calls it a kind of Messianic commitment to a redemptive mission: The United States was to be "a city . . . set on an hill," "a light unto the nations," exemplifying the blessings of liberty to the common man in less fortunate countries, and encouraging him to establish a liberal and democratic regime like unto ours.

So, in a sense, the United States can be said to be the most ideological of all nations—far more ideological than the Soviet Union, for instance, whose official political orthodoxy has never been able to sink deep roots, has never become a popular civil religion, a consensual orthodoxy, as has happened here. But, in another sense, the United States can also be said to have been one of the least ideological of nations. For, in addition to the philosophy of the Enlightenment, as incarnated in the Declaration of Independence, there was another and, for a long time, equally powerful political tradition that prevailed in the United States. This political tradition, rooted in centuries of British political experience and in British constitutional-juridical thought, found expression in the Constitution—a document that (unlike the contemporary French Revolutionary constitutions) was far more a lawyer's job of work than a social philosopher's. There is nothing particularly grand or visionary or utopian in the language of the Constitution. Its eloquence, where it exists, is the eloquence of British jurists as carried over and preserved in American legal education. And it proceeds to establish a mundane government based on a very prosaic estimate of men's capacities to subordinate passion to reason, prejudice to benevolence, self-interest to the public good.

For more than a century, these two traditions coexisted amiably if uneasily in American life. The exultant prophetic-utopian tradition was always the more popular; it represented, as it were, the vernacular of American political discourse. It was, and is, the natural rhetoric of the journalist and the political candidate, both of whom instinctively seek to touch the deepest springs of American sentiment. In contrast, the constitutional-legal tradition supplied the rhetoric for official occasions and for the official business of government—for Presidential messages, debates in Congress, Supreme Court decisions and the like.

Andrew Jackson, for example, was a radical populist in his time, and when he vetoed the bank bill in 1832, his followers celebrated this as "driving the money changers from the temple." He himself, however, in sending his message to the Senate, began it as follows:

The bill "to modify and continue" the act entitled "An Act to Incorporate the Subscribers to the Bank" was presented to me on the 4th July instant. Having considered it with that solemn regard to the principles of the Constitution which the day was calculated to inspire, and come to the conclusion that it ought not to become a law, I herewith return it to the Senate, in which it originated, with my objections.

A bank of the United States is in many respects convenient for the Government and useful to the people. Entertaining this opinion, and deeply impressed with the belief that some of the powers and privileges possessed by the existing bank are unauthorized by the Constitution, subversive of the rights of the states, and dangerous to the liberties of the people, I felt it my duty at an early period of my Administration to call the attention of Congress to the practicability of organizing an institution continuing all its advantages and obviating these objections. I sincerely regret that in the act before me I can perceive none of those modifications of the bank charter which are necessary, in my opinion, to make it compatible with justice, with sound policy, or with the Constitution of our country.

This "high" mode of discourse—without cant, without demagogy, without bombast—was then thought to be the normal way in which the American government should engage in public conversation with its own people or with the world at large. Concurrently, the political vernacular was infused with a declamatory passion. John L. O'Sullivan, a Jacksonian Democrat journalist who subsequently became a leading popular exponent of the United States' "Manifest Destiny" to expand over the entire continent, composed an endless stream of demagogic-prophetic editorials. They are perfect specimens of their type. Thus he wrote in 1839:

The far-reaching, the boundless future, will be the era of American greatness. In its magnificent domain of space and time, the nation of many nations is destined to manifest to mankind the excellence of divine principles, to establish on earth the noblest temple ever dedicated to the worship of the Most High—the Sacred and the True. Its floor shall be a hemisphere. . . .

And so on and so forth. The public lapped it up, and the Fourth of July orations continued to serve it up. But if one turns to the official statements of American foreign policy—statements by Presidents and Secretaries of State—one finds almost nothing of this sort. From George Washington to William McKinley, practically all such statements are sober and measured formulations of "sound policy," composed by constitutional lawyers who felt the need to argue the merits of their cases before the bar of rational and informed opinion. It is rare for any kind of breathless utopian or shrill prophetic notes to be sounded. Even at the outbreak of the Spanish-American

War, when jingoistic rhetoric was deafening in its persistence and intensity, President McKinley's War Message to Congress was a lawyer's brief, arguing the legality of American actions, emphasizing their moderate and prudent qualities, outlining the material issues involved, and offering only a minimum of that "high idealism" that has since become obligatory in Presidential prose.

 Sometime around the turn of the century, the impact of the Populist and Progressive movements combined to establish the vernacular utopian-prophetic rhetoric as the official rhetoric of American statesmen. It happened gradually, and it was not until the nineteen-thirties that the victory of the vernacular was complete and unchallengeable. But it also happened with a kind of irresistible momentum, as the egalitarian, "democratic" temper of the American people remorselessly destroyed the last vestiges of the neo-Whiggish, "republican" cast of mind. By now, we no longer find it in any way odd that American Presidents should sound like demagogic journalists of yesteryear. Indeed, we would take alarm and regard them as eccentric if they sounded like anything else.

III

The effects of this transformation have been momentous, though not much noticed or commented upon. High-flown double-talk has become the normal jargon of American government. This flatters and soothes the citizenry, but at the same time engenders a permanent credibility gap; instead of paying attention to what the government literally says—a waste of anyone's time—we expend much energy trying to figure out what the government really means. Official or quasi-official state documents, for the historian of today, have become trivial, superficial, and unreliable sources of information. No historian of Abraham Lincoln's period would dare minimize the importance of what he said during his debates with Douglas or in his two inaugural addresses; no historian of the nineteen-sixties would bother paying nearly as close attention to the public words of John F. Kennedy, Lyndon B. Johnson, or Richard M. Nixon. Our public rhetoric has become largely ritualistic—resounding utopian clichés that obfuscate a presumed "inside story" our reporters are always snuffling after.

The kinds of dangers this situation creates in the area of American foreign policy have been noted by some critics. Hans J. Morgenthau has pointed out that the closer we get to the founding fathers, the more sensible, the more forthright, the more realistic are our official statements of foreign policy. Conversely, the more we approach the present, the windier and more meaningless they become. Even our vocabulary becomes corrupted. The countries of Asia and Africa and South America used to be "poor"; in the course of the past 20 years they became first "underdeveloped," and now "less-developed." Plain language that accords with reality has become positively offensive to our sensibilities.

The corruption of plain language has been accompanied by —one might even say it has resulted in—the corruption of plain speaking. No Secretary of State can today describe the governments of Greece or Peru or Bolivia or Spain or Argentina or Egypt as what they obviously are: military dictatorships. It would cause a diplomatic row; these nations have become so accustomed to our hypocritical double-talk that they would sense some sinister intentions in any deviation from it. Similarly, no Secretary of State could ever say that a particular regime—for example, the Communist government of China— is abhorrent to our own political values but that we are nevertheless prepared to have diplomatic relations with it and to do business with it, since it suits our national interests at this time to do so. No, he has to announce the dawn of a new diplomatic era, a giant step to world peace, and all the rest of that nonsense. It is nonsense because he has no grounds whatever for believing this, and it is altogether possible that a United States-China *rapprochement* could heighten the possibility of war in some parts of the world—on the Russian-Chinese border, for instance, or the India-Pakistan frontier.

A particularly striking instance of how impossible it is for simple and incontestable truths to be uttered in high places is provided by the rhetoric in which our foreign aid programs are cocooned. Never mind, for the moment, whether these programs are good or bad, overly generous or terribly niggardly. The one certain fact about these programs is that they cannot even begin to do what they promise: namely, in our lifetime to bring the standard of living of the "less-developed" countries closer to the American-West European standard. *Nothing* can do that. If we allow that India's economy might grow at an uninterruptedly rapid rate (say, 10 per cent) for the next 29 years, and assume that the American growth rate will sustain itself at the modest level of 5 per cent during that period, then—because of the initial huge disparity—by the magic year 2000 the gap between the Indian and American per capita income will, in absolute terms, be *greater* than it is today. The notion, therefore, that any significant portion of the "third world" can even begin to "catch up" to the West in the next generation is an absurdity. Indeed, given the fact that "less-developed" countries are dependent on fairly high growth rates in the United States and Europe for their own economic growth, the probability is that they will not "catch up" anytime in the next several generations, and there is a good chance they may never "catch up" at all.

Yet, who can say this? No United States government official can—he would be denounced as a sour pessimist and driven from office. No official or political leader in a "less-developed" country can—he would be denounced as a traitor and driven from office. So, no one says it. Instead we talk grandly about "economic development" in a deceitful and misleading way. The inevitable result is that the economic growth which does take place in poorer lands—and many of them are doing quite well, by historical standards—is universally denounced as "inadequate." A more perfect recipe for permanent political instability in these nations cannot be imagined.

Worst of all, the corruption of language and speech results in the corruption of thought. One has only to observe the hearings before the Senate or House Foreign Relations Committees to realize that, once you surrender the liberty to speak plainly, you lose the capacity to think clearly. Sustained hypocrisy is one of the most intolerable regimens for the mind: In the end, you find yourself believing yourself and taking your own empty rhetoric seriously.

Thus, it is one of the oldest and truest proverbs in international relations that, under certain circumstances, the enemy of your enemy becomes your friend—even if, had you a freer choice, you would never want such a friend at all. All nations operate on this essential principle, and the United States is no exception. Yet one can read the testimony of government officials and "expert witnesses" for years on end without coming across a clear enunciation of it as the rationale for some aspect of American policy. We have a terrible time explaining to ourselves that, while we have an instinctive, democratic (and healthy) dislike for dictatorships, we have precious little control over the way other peoples govern or misgovern themselves. Our relations with other nations, and theirs with us, are determined for the most part by calculations of mutual advantage. One gets the distinct impression that our government is not only ashamed to admit it engages in such calculations—it actually is reluctant to engage in them, except under the random pressure of necessity which it then perceives as an "emergency." We have been telling ourselves for so long that our foreign policy proceeds on quite other principles that we have lost the art and skill of coping with the principles that do, in fact, prevail. Our statesmen are always reacting to reality as an "emergency," in an *ad hoc* fashion, and having at the same time to invent a fancy, "idealistic" motive for the most prosaic and practical actions.

Witness the typically American fuss and furor in recent months over whether the elections in South Vietnam were truly democratic—and if they were not, what we should then be doing about it. The assumption seems to be that the original purpose of our intervention in Vietnam was to establish parliamentary government there, and that the absence of such government presents us with a crisis. But this is a childish assumption. We did not intervene for any such purpose. (At least I hope we didn't—I can't bring myself to believe that the men who make our foreign policy were quite that idiotic.) Our intervention was to help establish a friendly, relatively stable regime which could coexist peacefully with the other nations of Southeast Asia. If such a regime prefers corrupt elections to the kind of overt military dictatorship that more usually prevails in that part of the world, this is its own affair. It constitutes no problem for us—any more than does the fact that Communist China prefers to manage with no elections at all. Our relations with both of these Asian nations are based mainly on considerations of international stability—on maintaining a version of international stability acceptable to us—not on how they go about governing themselves.

To be sure, being an American I am keenly aware of the merits of representative government, and I do hope that the Vietnamese (South *and* North) will at some time recognize these merits. But I am also aware that these merits do not automatically commend themselves to all nations, at all times, everywhere. Our foreign relations, therefore, must of necessity be more concerned with the external policies of any particular nation than with its internal form of government. This is as true for South Vietnam as it is for China or Russia or Cuba. We are perfectly free, as Americans, to be critical of, or even to have contempt for, their systems of government. But, as Americans, we are also free not to live there, and we are therefore bound to be more interested in their behavior to others than in their behavior to themselves. I think most Americans would subscribe to this common-sense proposition. But it is not a proposition we would permit our spokesman at the United Nations to enunciate. And there do seem to be many eminent Americans—notably, an entire class of liberal journalists—who have been utterly bewitched by our official platitudes. These men and women, after traveling freely throughout South Vietnam, heap scorn upon its "corrupt" democracy. They then make a strictly guided tour of China to return aglow with admiration! One can only assume that such men and women think it natural to judge our allies by quite utopian standards, but are ready to give unfriendly nations the benefit of every possible doubt.

IV

But it is not only in foreign affairs that our government proceeds by utopian promises of future benefits and hypocritical explanations of actual performance. Our entire domestic policy is suffused with this same self-defeating duality. Thus, as a domestic counterpart to a "war to end all wars," we have in the past decade launched a "war to end poverty." The very title of that crusade reveals a mindless enthusiasm which could only lead to bitter disillusionment.

There are two ways of defining poverty: in absolute terms or relative terms. The absolute definition, involving estimates by government agencies of an adequate diet, adequate shelter, adequate clothing for an average family, is relatively easy to make. It is also largely meaningless in a context of "the abolition of poverty." To see just how meaningless it is, one has only to report that the majority of welfare families in New York City are now above the officially determined "poverty line." Have we ceased regarding them—have they ceased regarding themselves—as poor? Of course not. If you take a family with an annual income of $3,800 and, one way or another, increase this income to $4,500, you have helped them somewhat—but you certainly have not abolished their poverty, as grandly promised. The consequence is that the modest but real improvement is obliterated by an exacerbated sense of "relative deprivation."

Most people, when they hear talk of "abolishing poverty," inevitably and immediately have in mind a substantial relative improvement, not merely a modest absolute one. They think in terms of elevating all those below the United States median family income—approximately $9,500 a year—to the vicinity of this level. That does not *look* like such an unreasonable goal. After all, families that make $9,500 a year have to watch their nickels and dimes if they are to make ends meet. (Ask them, and they'll tell you—and they'll be telling the truth.) But this is one of those cases where appearances are deceptive, and what looks like a reasonable goal is in fact utopian. To achieve it would require either the creation of new income or the redistribution of existing income to the tune of perhaps $200-billion a year.* This is simply impossible; there is no policy,

* One must remember: If you establish a guaranteed minimum family income of, say, $8,000 a year, you are then faced with the problems of those who work to earn $9,000 or $10,000. Are they to labor for a measly $1,000 or $2,000 a year? You cannot ask that, and they would not tolerate it if you

however "radical," that could come close to accomplishing this. We may be an "affluent" society by historical standards, but we are not nearly that affluent. (Total corporate profits last year, after taxes, were well under $50-billion). Yet who dares to say so? Instead, our politicians (and our journalists and professors, too) persist in holding up this impossible ideal, with the quite predictable effect of making people intensely dissatisfied with social policies that achieve (though never easily) smaller increments to their income or smaller improvements of their condition.

The upshot of this state of affairs is that any American who, today, passes his working life in moving from $4,000 a year to an ultimate $9,500 is regarded as a pathetic victim of circumstances, a prisoner in a "dead-end job." Yet just about half of all Americans pass their working lives in this way, and are going to do so regardless of anything said or done in Washington. All that our utopian rhetoric can do is to convince them that the normal working-class experience—the *inevitable* working-class experience, which would be as common in a socialist United States as in a capitalist United States—is a fate akin to degradation.

V

Or take our "welfare problem." Welfare policy in the United States is based on a very simple—and enormously flattering—thesis about American human nature. The thesis consists of the following propositions: (1) all Americans are highly motivated to work as a means of improving their material condi-

---

did. So you have to make some kind of supplementary payments to these families, too. And *then* you are faced with the problem of those who work to earn $12,000 a year—and so on, and on. It is this "ripple effect" that makes the guaranteed income, at any level above a ludicrously low one, such a fantastically expensive proposition.

tion; (2) those Americans who seem not to be so motivated are suffering from temporary "psychological deprivation" as a result of poverty, bad housing, bad health and so on; (3) improve their material environment and the "normal" impulse to self-betterment will automatically assert itself. It is a plausible thesis to our American ears. Moreover, there is enough historical experience behind it to suggest it is not entirely false. Only, when applied indiscriminately, it turns out to be more false than true. Some people, whether in the United States or elsewhere, respond according to this formula. A great many others, however, do not. It turns out there are lots of people in this world, including a great many Americans, who do not fill the American prescription for "human nature."

Once you think about it, this is not really surprising. For what our high expectations and our high-flown rhetoric overlook—are bound to overlook, because they are so high-flying —is that we are for the most part talking about motivation directed toward *small* improvements. You can motivate almost anyone to become a millionaire, if the possibility is offered; but that possibility rarely is. And it is another thing entirely to motivate people to move from a badly paying situation (say, casual laborer) to a slightly better-paying but also more arduous one (say, laundry worker or drill-press operator). That is the kind of grim motivation you need to get "self-sustained" economic growth, whether among nations or among individuals. Not all human beings are born with this kind of grim motivation—which is just as well, I'd say, since the earth would then be a pretty dreary, if industrious, place.

In the absence of such ingrained motivation, the usual way we motivate people—even in America—has been by adding the spur of necessity to the offer of modest opportunity. That small improvement has to make a real difference: the difference between squalor and poverty, or between poverty and minimum comfort. These "little" differences—almost invisible to the middle-class eye, and never taken seriously by middle-class reformers—are absolutely crucial to the self-discipline and self-respect of ordinary working people. They need to be very much aware of the costs of not achieving them, if the achievement is to have any merit or meaning in their eyes.

I suspect that all of this sounds petty, and sordid, and mean-spirited. We are accustomed to thinking about poor people, and about ways of helping poor people, in more elevated terms than these. And so we introduce something like our present welfare policies. These policies, at one swoop, abolish all those important little differences in achievement. They generously offer all poor people more in the way of welfare than they can get for their unskilled labor on the open market—more, often, than they would earn at the legal minimum wage. Naturally, these people, not being fanatics about work, move onto the welfare rolls in very large numbers. To be precise, their wives and children are pushed onto welfare. The men themselves drift away from their homes, demoralized by the knowledge that their function as breadwinner has been preempted by welfare. These men then merge into the shadows of street-corner society—superfluous men, subsisting by casual labor or casual crime, men whose families are materially no worse off for their absence and would be no better off for their presence. Has there ever been a more ingenious formula for the destruction of poor families? Indeed, one can fairly speculate how many middle-class families would hang together if the family suffered no financial inconvenience as a result of the husband's vanishing.

Welfare is wreaking devastation on the American poor—making the child fatherless, the wife husbandless, the husband useless. We see this "welfare explosion" happening and, disconcerted, turn this calamity of our own creation into an indictment of our social order.

Once you have put people on welfare, it is a nasty business

getting them off. You can either (1) cut welfare rates so as to make it distinctly worth their while to go to work, or (2) keep welfare rates high for those truly unable to work—the aged, the sick, the disabled, the unemployed—but have a severe, suspicious welfare bureaucracy that defines its mission as getting as many of the rest off the rolls as is possible. Neither alternative is attractive, though the latter seems to me considerably more humane. (Its social consequences are also likely to be beneficial, since we know that families on welfare tend to develop social pathologies: they produce relatively more criminals, drug addicts, alcoholics, illegitimate children, etc.). But the second option does involve our taking a more realistic view of human nature and of human motivation—and this we are most unlikely to do. So we shall either veer toward the first course, indiscriminately penalizing all welfare recipients in the name of "economy," or, more probably, we shall simply stagger on until some kind of social explosion takes place.

It really is a curious phenomenon we are witnessing: a nation preferring to live under a perpetual, self-inflicted indictment of "social injustice," and amidst an ever-swelling and ever-more-demoralized population on the dole, rather than revise its utterly fanciful and utopian idea of human nature. There cannot have been many instances in history of such high-minded masochism. We may even be the first.

VI

What is true of welfare is even more blatantly true of our other social problems. Our utopian illusions always are preferred to realistic assessments of human beings, and to the world in which real human beings live.

In no area are the ravages of American utopianism more visible than in education. Here intellectual fads and fashions reign supreme, all of them exultant in promise, all of them negligible in accomplishment. Our professional educators today are perpetually and enthusiastically engaged in deception and self-deception, in part out of necessity, in part because they actually feel this is their "responsibility." We know a great deal about the relationship between schools and academic achievement. But it is the rare educator who dares to say what we know, to challenge the sovereign platitudes as to what a school can do to the young people who enter it.

We know from the Coleman Report and other studies, for instance, that there is practically no correlation between the physical plant of our schools and the academic achievement of our students. We may desire new, well-equipped schools for all sorts of reasons. They may be good reasons; they may even, in some vague sense, qualify as "educational" reasons; but they are not academic reasons. Students learn as well in old, decrepit school buildings as in new, shiny ones; or they learn as little in the latter as in the former. Middle-class parents who think they are improving their children's academic potential by sending them to a brand-new school with a fine library, a sumptuous gymnasium, a lovely lunchroom are kidding themselves. So are slum parents who think that their children's academic potential is weakened by old buildings, cramped gymnasiums (or no gymnasium), shabby lunchrooms, paltry libraries (or no library). What determines a child's academic achievement is his genetic endowment plus the values and motivation he acquires at home. All the rest may have significant consequences for a child's life style, his appearance, perhaps (and I myself regard this as the most important function of schools) what we call his "character." But it will have little to do with his academic achievement.

Even class size turns out to have nothing to do with academic achievement. There are, in my view, good reasons—

having to do with the role of the teacher as an "adult model" in the process of "character formation"—for preferring smaller classes to larger ones. But they are not academic reasons. Whether a class has twenty pupils or thirty or even forty simply doesn't matter. Students who do well in small classes will do well in large ones. Students who do poorly in large classes will do no better in small ones. This subject has been studied to death by generations of educational researchers, and the results are conclusive.

Nevertheless, the educator who dares to utter these truths publicly is instantly classified as, at best, an eccentric. His opinions are marked as "controversial"—though they are not—whereas an educator who stresses the academic importance of new schools and small classes is simply seen as tediously "sound." Every year, in New York City, a furious debate breaks out when the statistics on the reading levels in the city schools are made available. These statistics always show that the average reading levels in New York's schools are lower than the national average—and they usually show that, with each year, they are steadily falling further below the national average. The publication of these figures always shocks, always provokes front-page news stories. But far from being shocking, these statistics aren't even newsworthy, since they are perfectly predictable. The reason that reading scores in New York's schools are falling away from the national average is that an ever-increasing percentage of our students come from very low-income families that are also broken, transient, and generally problem-ridden families. The children in these families show low academic aptitude. We insist that our schools "do something" about increasing the academic ability of these youngsters, and our educational leaders furiously institute every gimmick they can think of with the assurance that this time they will turn the trick.

Our insistence is as unreasonable as their assurances are worthless. The schools cannot perform this sociological miracle—which, if it is to take place at all, will happen in the family, at home, over a period of time that is rarely shorter than a couple of generations. As such poor families move up the economic and social ladder, as their home life becomes more stable and the family concern for education becomes more emphatic, the student's academic performance improves. In individual cases, "miracles" do certainly occur. But in the mass, statistical probability reigns supreme—and the schools play no role in the calculations. If you want to estimate the chances of a student doing well or badly in school, give him a physical examination, look at his home, and give him an intelligence test. But don't bother him with questions about his school—it is of no importance for *this* purpose.

And how do we react to this fact? With furious indignation, usually. So, as the school's impotence to satisfy our unrealistic demands becomes ever more clear, we shall—it is already beginning to happen—abolish reading scores and reading tests on the grounds that they are irrelevant to eventual academic achievement. This monumental act of self-deception will, of course, fool nobody and change nothing. But it will certainly be hailed by professional educators as a marvelous innovation.

Of late, many educators have waxed enthusiastic over the educational possibilities of small mixed classes, with the older students helping to instruct the younger, and with every student proceeding "at his own pace." This is, of course, exactly what used to happen in the "little red schoolhouse." I have always been fond of the little red schoolhouse and was unhappy that, after a determined campaign over many decades, our professional educators succeeded in outlawing it. If they now wish to reinstitute it, I certainly have no objections. But

I find it more than a little nauseating that they should now present it as a brilliant educational innovation which will solve all our educational problems. And I find it unconscionable that these educators can be so easy in mind and spirit about their newest fad when the huge educational parks which—only yesterday—they insisted were absolutely necessary, are just now coming into existence.

A good principal can always make a *small* difference in the academic power of a school—and a small difference is surely better than none at all. A dedicated teacher may make a big difference to *a few* students—and this difference is to be treasured. But none of this satisfies us. We insist that our schools fulfill impossible dreams—and so they pretend to be able to do this (given a larger budget, of course). As a result, the world of American education is at the moment suffused with charlatanism, and anyone with a sober word to say is encouraged to go elsewhere.

VII

The consequence of this public insistence on a utopian vision of man, history, and society is that our public life is shot through with a permanent streak of hysteria. We are constantly indicting ourselves, denouncing our nation, lamenting our fate. Indeed, an entire profession has emerged—we call it "the media"—which has taken upon itself the responsibility for leading this chorus. Just imagine what our TV commentators and "news analysts" would do with a man who sought elected office with the promise that, during his tenure, he hoped to effect some small improvements in our condition. They would ridicule him into oblivion. In contrast, they are very fond of someone like John Lindsay, who will settle for only the finest and most glowing goals. Public figures in our society get credit for their utopian rhetoric—for their "charisma," as we now say—and only demerits if they emphasize their (necessarily modest) achievements.

Every society needs ideals and self-criticism and some prophetic admonition. It needs these to correct its "natural" tendency toward smugness, inertia and parochial self-satisfaction. But when the countertendency toward insistent self-dissatisfaction becomes overwhelming, then such a society is in grave trouble. The capacity for contentment is atrophied. So is the willingness to see things as they really are, and then to improve them in a matter-of-fact way. This matter-of-fact way may involve some quite "radical" reforms and innovations. But if they are to be successful, they must be sensible as well as radical. They must be aware that our ideals cannot simply be imposed on the real world, but must have some original congruence with it.

We certainly do have it in our power to make improvements in the human estate. But to think we have it in our power to change people so as to make the human estate wonderfully better than it is, remarkably different from what it is, and in very short order, is to assume that this generation of Americans can do what no other generation in all of human history could accomplish. American though I be, I cannot bring myself to accept this arrogant assumption. I think, rather, that by acting upon this assumption we shall surely end up making our world worse than it need have been.

73 74 75 10 9 8 V 6 5 4 3 2